Phoenix, Scottsdale, Sedona & Central Arizona

Phoenix, Scottsdale, Sedona & Central Arizona

A Great Destination

Christine K. Bailey

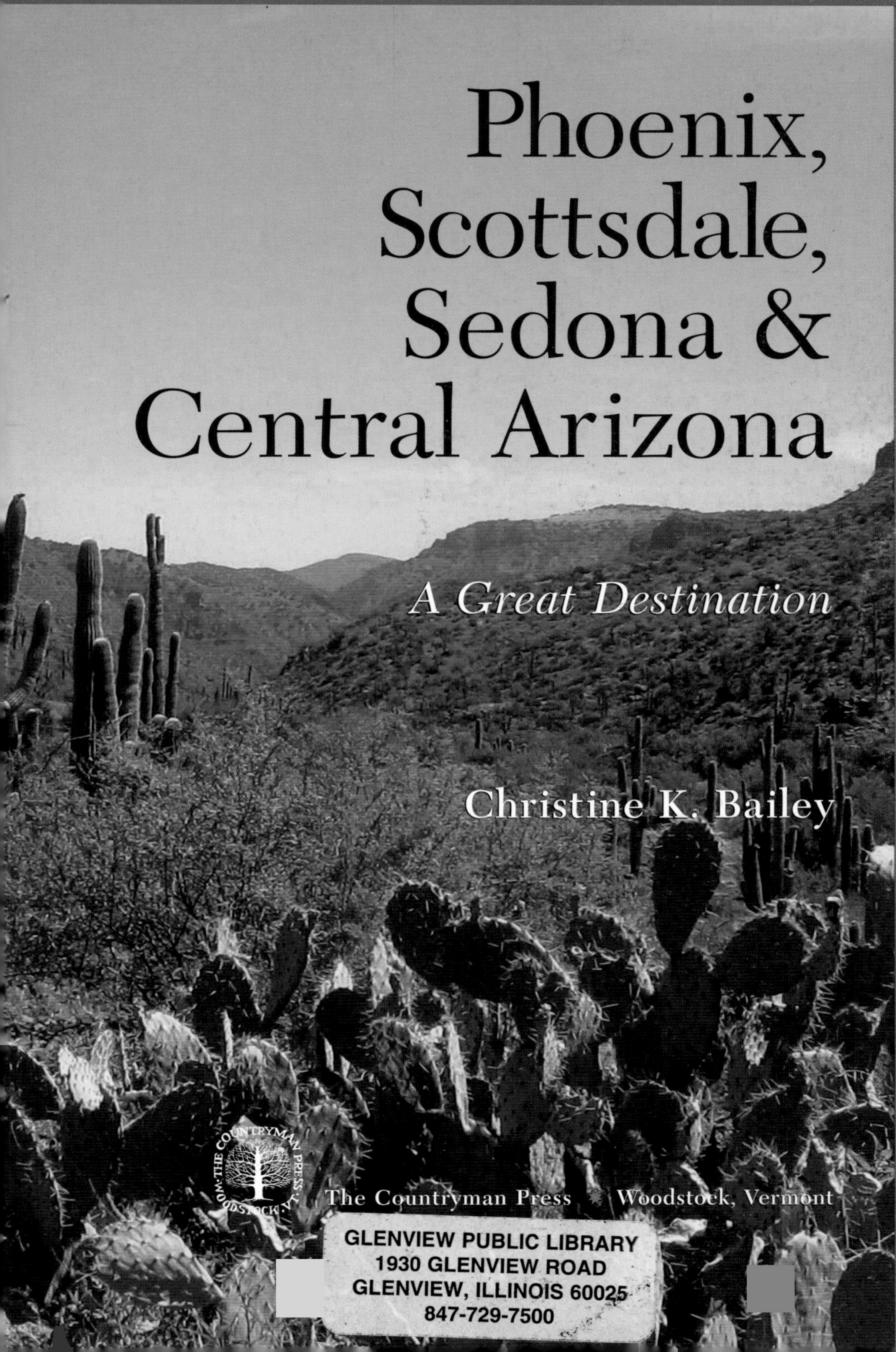

The Countryman Press   Woodstock, Vermont

SECOND EDITION

Copyright © 2011 by Christine K. Bailey

Phoenix, Scottsdale, Sedona, & Central Arizona
ISBN 978-1-58157-044-1

Interior photographs by the author unless otherwise specified
Maps by Erin Greb Cartography, © The Countryman Press
Book design by Joanna Bodenweber
Composition by Eugenie S. Delaney

Published by The Countryman Press, P.O. Box 748, Woodstock, VT 05091
Distributed by W. W. Norton & Company, Inc., 500 Fifth Avenue, New York, NY 10110
Printed in the United States of America

10 9 8 7 6 5 4 3 2 1

To Matt, for his love and support,
and for his faith in me.

Acknowledgments

The original edition of this book is still very much a foundation for this one; the people who influenced the content you'll find in its pages are still here cheering me on (husband, children, sister, parents, and friends). I am forever grateful for your love and support.

To a few new colleagues who have helped me make the leap to full-time writer; five amazing women writers who encouraged me to make writing an everyday part of my life: Audrey RL Wyatt, CL Coons, Robin Kramme, Terri Weeding, and Wendy Marshall; to my fellow Arizona travel and food writers who simultaneously inspire and challenge me: Jackie Dishner, Teresa Bitler, and Geri Koeppel (whose sidebars you'll get to read in this edition); and to all of the others—writers, editors, chefs, teachers, dancers, artists, business owners—I've met on trips, at the coffee shop, doing business, via Facebook, and on Twitter—thank you for making a place in this world for doing what you love. It makes it easier for the rest of us to follow our passions.

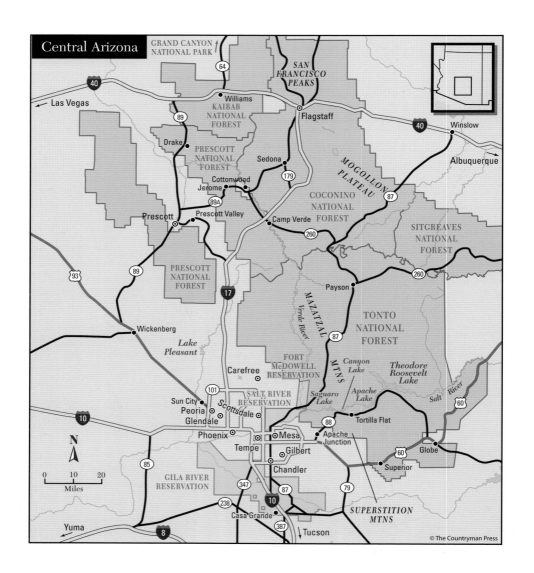

Contents

Introduction

If living in Arizona since 1998 doesn't make me a native, then the 20-plus years of listening to my father—born in Tucson in 1955 at St. Mary's Hospital—does. Less than a year old, living on a plot of land as wild as any desert you'll see today, with a swamp cooler to stave off the humid monsoon weather, he started forming the impressions that he would later pass on to his midwestern family. It would take him almost 43 years (with mere visits in between) to return for good—and in the process to bring all of us with him.

He instilled in us a sense of adventure, an excitement for exploration, and an appreciation for all things Arizonan—from the snakes, spiders, and scorpions to the pungent smell of wet creosote after a summer rain. Both of my sons, born in Chandler, Arizona, in 2002 and 2005 respectively, already know that while all snakes are amazing creatures, we cannot always tell which ones are poisonous and which ones aren't—and so we step around them with respect and awe. They are our neighbors.

In a state where climate is considered a commodity, it is no surprise that Arizona attracts more than 35 million visitors each year. From border to border, our state boasts one natural wonder after another—the Petrified Forest in the Painted Desert, the Grand Canyon, Organ Pipe National Forest, Kartchner Caverns, and Tonto Natural Bridge State Park, to name only a few. Even residents of Arizona—a whopping 30 percent of Arizona's tourists each year—travel the state on weekends searching for something new to do and see. And they are never disappointed. Art galleries, museums, historic sites, resorts, restaurants, natural parks, monuments, and shops stretch from the Arizona–Mexico border north through Tombstone, Bisbee, Tucson, Coolidge, Casa Grande, Chandler, Tempe, Glendale, Payson, Yuma, Prescott, Sedona, Camp Verde, Flagstaff, Winslow, Lake Havasu, and Page—and this list is but a sampling of the cities and towns and landmarks, each rich with history, culture, and geographic charm, nestled among the foothills, mountains, and deserts that cover the state.

But perhaps the Valley of the Sun—home to Phoenix, the fifth-largest city in the United States and the capital of Arizona—can be considered representative of all that is Arizonan. Located in the heart of the Sonoran Desert, within half a day's drive of any given point of interest, the Valley is a multifaceted jewel of emerald golf courses, sapphire skies, and the amber and ruby rays of breathtaking sunsets.

Currently thousands of people flock monthly to the Phoenix metro area alone, and the famous saying of John B. L. Soule (or Horace Greeley—wherever you may have "heard" it first)—"Go west young man, and grow up with the country"—still rings true. They are the young, the old, and the active, and perhaps they, too, have found what they've been looking for. With so much to offer, Arizona might just be your little spot of happiness. So whether you're here for a romantic vacation, visiting for a three-day conference with only a couple of hours to spare, or here to stay, we hope that you find this book full of possibility and your time here an adventure.

The Way This Book Works

For your convenience, this book has been divided into regions and cities within the Phoenix metropolitan area—known to locals as the Valley of the Sun. You will find nine chapters: History, Transportation, Phoenix, Scottsdale, Tempe and the East Valley, Glendale and the West Valley, Sedona, Side Trips, and Information, which provide important details to help you better enjoy your stay in Arizona as well as great online resources and books to supplement what you find in this book.

But wait, we added something new to the second edition: the 48-hour itinerary. If you're only in town for a few days, you can catch the highlights that each area covered in this book has to offer. We also added and updated maps, provided new side bars, tips and suggestions and included "if you like this . . . you'll like this" recommendations throughout the book. The content and layout has been re-designed to help you navigate the book and the area more easily.

The History and Transportation chapters provide you with background information on Greater Phoenix and tips on how to navigate it, respectively. The Phoenix chapter covers the city of Phoenix and all it has to offer, from traveling downtown to visiting the Heard Museum. The chapter on Scottsdale highlights information about Frank Lloyd Wright's Taliesin West, shopping and spa options, and what you can expect in downtown Scottsdale. Tempe and the East Valley targets things to do around Arizona State University's Tempe campus, including its various museums, as well as tips about navigating the Mill Avenue District and what you'll find in Chandler, Gilbert, or Mesa. Glendale and the West Valley features tips on how to take a tour of University of Phoenix Stadium and what you can do in Historic Downtown Glendale, plus it reveals some of the latest spring training additions to the West Valley.

The Sedona and Side Trips chapters include information, maps, and best bets for exploring the rest of the state. As a top tourist destination in the country, Sedona has so many wonderful things to offer that it warranted a chapter of its own. But don't underestimate the charm and draw of the old mining towns of Jerome and Bisbee or the artistry and historical significance of Tubac. These little communities have reinvented themselves as artist magnets, and you will find information about them in our Side Trips chapter. Since Arizona is the Grand Canyon State, we thought it important to include information about a trip to one of the world's seven natural wonders. You will also read about Payson (home of the world's oldest continuous rodeo), Tucson (Spanish influences abound in the Old Pueblo), and the Pima Air and Space Museum.

In Information, you'll find important phone numbers, an overview of our weather and surviving in it, and a list of great books by Arizonans and about Arizona. You'll also find online resources like iPhone applications for traveling in Arizona and blogs and Twitter feeds to follow for the latest and greatest tips on what to see and do here.

FINDING YOUR HOME BASE IN THE VALLEY

Most people tend to stay and visit in one particular part of the Valley, so our goal was to create an easily navigable book that provides important information about where to stay, where to eat, and what to do in the particular area you've chosen. Here's a little overview of the Valley of the Sun to help you decide where to begin.

You'll want to plan your stay in Phoenix around what you want to see and do while you're here. While the Valley has become more easily accessible with the recent expansions of Loops 101 and 202, it still pays to stay where you plan to spend most of your time. If you're visiting Arizona State University's Tempe Campus, Tempe, South Scottsdale, and the airport area are good choices. Not only do these areas provide inexpensive hotel rates and easy access to campus, but they are also minutes away from the Desert Botanical Garden, Phoenix Zoo, Papago Park, and Phoenix South Mountain Preserve. You are also close to downtown Phoenix and downtown Scottsdale; combined with the Mill Avenue District, you have a variety of shopping, dining, and entertainment choices.

Interested in stylish boutiques, first-class restaurants, spectacular golf, and the best spas? Try the fashionable Biltmore District/Camelback Corridor in the area where Phoenix, Scottsdale, and Paradise Valley converge. Here you'll find resorts like Camelback Inn, Arizona Biltmore, the Ritz-Carlton Phoenix, The Phoenician, Montelucia, Sanctuary on Camelback, and Royal Palms Resort and Spa. Check both the Phoenix and Scottsdale chapters for where to stay in this particular area (resorts are listed according to their post office addresses). In addition to the golf courses and spas, visitors enjoy hiking Camelback Mountain and Piestewa Peak or shopping at Biltmore Fashion Park. The district's close proximity to Old Town Scottsdale on the east and Piestewa Peak Parkway on the west means additional restaurant and entertainment options.

The Gainey Ranch neighborhood in Scottsdale is surrounded by golf courses, country clubs, spas, and boutiques. You will find the Hyatt Regency Scottsdale Resort and Spa at Gainey Ranch set against the breathtaking McDowell Mountains. Just north of there are the Westin Kierland and Fairmont Scottsdale Princess as well as The Players' Club (TPC), home of the greatest show on grass: the Waste Management Open (once the Phoenix Open). Kierland Commons features a variety of shopping and dining options in an old main-street-style setting. Just north of the 101 in north Phoenix, tourists enjoy staying at one of the larger Valley resorts, the JW Marriott Desert Ridge—technically in Phoenix, this resort is known for Vegas-style flair, beautiful golf courses, and a pampering spa. Plus, this area now boasts the Musical Instrument Museum—the only museum of its kind to showcase musical instruments from more than two hundred countries and territories from around the world.

Squaw Peak Lawn, the Arizona Biltmore, Phoenix

A stay in downtown Scottsdale in March means spring training and the San Francisco Giants. If you're an art fan, downtown features 125 art galleries, a weekly arts walk, Scottsdale Center for the Performing Arts, and the Scottsdale Museum of Contemporary Art. The area is home to urban-style boutique hotels—Hotel Valley Ho, Hotel Theodore, and W Scottsdale, but you'll also find several affordable brands that give you easy access to the hundreds of shops, art galleries, and restaurants in the area. In addition to the Main Street, Marshall Way, Old Town, and Fifth Avenue shopping and arts districts (where a free trolley service circulates daily), you can visit Scottsdale Fashion Square and the Waterfront. These locales feature local shops and restaurants just north of the downtown area.

Others may enjoy a stay in the East Valley, which tends to have a more relaxed atmosphere along with affordable accommodations, the historic Crowne Plaza San Marcos Golf Resort, charming restaurants like the Crackers & Co. Café in Tempe or Joe's Real BBQ in Gilbert, and shopping at Chandler Fashion Center in Chandler and Tempe Marketplace in Tempe. Golf lovers will find some spectacular courses, like the Ocotillo Golf Resort in Chandler, at great rates. Activities include hiking or horseback riding in the Usery Mountains north of Mesa or visiting Goldfield—a touristy old mining town in the shadows of the oft-photographed Superstition Mountains—tubin' down the Salt River, or shopping Mesa's Main Street or Chandler's town square. Visitors enjoy the Mesa Contemporary Arts museum, and kids love the "dinosaur museum"—as local children call the Arizona Museum of Natural History. RV owners might like Mesa and Apache Junction, which offer a variety of choices.

If you're here antiquing or to see the Arizona Cardinals or the Phoenix Coyotes, try the West Valley. Historic Downtown Glendale is home to some of the best antiques stores and local restaurants. Enjoy the weekly arts walk, annual events like the Glendale Chocolate Affaire or the Glendale Jazz and Blues Festival, and the state-of-the-art technologically inspired shopping at Westgate City Center adjacent to the new University of Phoenix Stadium—home of the Arizona Cardinals. If you're looking to retire, any of the choices will do, but Sun City and Sun City West in the northwest Valley have several resort-style active adult communities, as do Goodyear and Litchfield farther south. Peoria features the Smithsonian-sponsored Challenger Space Center and Lake Pleasant Regional Park. Hike, camp, or horseback ride in the White Tank or Estrella mountains; golf at the Palm Valley Golf Club in Goodyear or Raven Golf Club at Verrado in Buckeye. Shopping can be found at Arrowhead Towne Center in Glendale or at the various shops and strip malls exploding throughout a quickly growing West Valley.

If you're here for a convention or prefer to stay in the very heart of things— downtown Phoenix offers everything from sports (the Diamondbacks and Phoenix Suns are within walking distance or at the very least a short drive) to arts and culture—Symphony Hall and the Herberger Theater are mere steps away from each other, and the Dodge and Orpheum theaters are close by, as are a variety of bars and restaurants. With the new additions to the Phoenix Civic Plaza and the thousand-room Sheraton Phoenix Downtown Hotel, more and more people are visiting the heart of the Valley. Still, downtown Phoenix tends to be laid-back; after 5 on weeknights it can be a quiet place, but there is plenty going on if you know where to look. Lines snake outside as hordes of people wait for a table at Pizzeria Bianco or a glass of wine at the adjacent Bar Bianco, both at the Heritage & Science Park. The Roosevelt Row District is up and coming with its late-night bars and restaurants (like Sens and The Roosevelt Tavern), art galleries, and the attention it receives on First Fridays (the downtown Phoenix version of an art walk). You can also shop, dine, or play in the downtown area's latest urban development—CityScape, located on the corner of First and Washington, or catch the same at the Arizona Center on Third Street and Van Buren.

Just north of the downtown area is considered midtown. With the METRO Light Rail running straight down Central Avenue, you now have easy access to the restaurants, shops, and attractions along the way, from the Heard Museum to the Phoenix Art Museum; from popular Phoenix restaurants with history like Durant's or Macayo's to brand-new trendy spots like Fez or Switch. Want to unwind after a busy day? Grab a drink and an appetizer at Cheuvront Restaurant & Wine Bar; the light rail will let you out, practically at their front door.

A well-chosen home base can enrich your experience, and the wonderful thing about most of these areas is that they are self-sufficient, offering a different combination of Arizona experiences. The mountains interspersed throughout the Valley mean it's but a short drive from just about anywhere to wandering paths, vigorous hikes, or escapes into the desert. Visitors can spend days exploring everything each area has to offer, from boutiques to art galleries, museums, big restaurants and little ones, theaters, mountains, golf courses, and spas.

We hope you enjoy your stay!

History

TAMING THE DESERT

Arizona is defined by its landscape, its weather, its temperatures, its large beauties, and its little charms. From the bold and indefinable beauty of the Grand Canyon to the buttery bloom of the saguaro cactus, Arizona encompasses untold natural marvels and undiscovered adventures. Arizona is blue skies and layered sunsets, tall mountains and sweeping plains, saguaro cacti and pine forests, raging waterfalls and dry riverbeds; it is ski resorts and saunas, rugged climbs and poolside naps—it is both the yin and the yang.

Defined by its mild winters and hot summers, its cool red-rock buttes and Sonoran Desert, central Arizona is no different. Many visitors from big cities like Chicago, New York, and Los Angeles are surprised to learn that they can drive 20 minutes to the South Mountain Preserve and lose themselves in 26,000 acres of desert and rolling hills. Or they can just as easily use those 20 minutes to reach downtown Phoenix and hear the Phoenix Symphony Orchestra, or watch a Broadway play, or see the Diamondbacks play at Chase Field. It is amazing how much of the city you can actually see—it's a spectacular view. This is a place where nature is still very much a part of the environment—the Valley of the Sun won't be losing its desert charm anytime soon.

If you're here to find chic, metropolitan experiences, don't bother—locals are known to wear shorts to Symphony Hall. If you've come to find that beautiful space between urban and rural—the carefully selected best of both worlds—then welcome to Arizona. We trust that you will find what you're looking for.

HOW THE LAND CAME TO BE

The land that forms our state was once part of the Sea of Cortez. Over billions of years, the waters receded, and the bare granite rock gave way beneath the ferocity of wind and rain, revealing layers of geological history and forming three distinct geographic zones—Basin and Range, Mountain, and Plateau.

The largest of these geographic systems—Basin and Range—covers the southwestern and south-central region of the state and encompasses Tucson and

Fast fact: Mount Humphreys measures 12,633 feet and is the highest of the San Francisco Peaks—a series of prehistoric volcanoes. For more volcanic remnants, check out the Sunset Crater Volcano National Monument (928-526-0502; www.nps.gov/sucr).

Did you know? *Arizona Highways* magazine, owned by the state of Arizona and managed by the department of transportation, published its first issue in 1925.

Phoenix in the Sonoran Desert. It comprises alternating spaces of flat desert and mountaintops that reach high enough off the desert floor to support forests of ponderosa pine. The second largest system, Mountain, divides northern and southern Arizona. This higher elevation is cooler and lusher. Here you'll find meadows and thick forests; the picturesque towns of Flagstaff, Prescott, Jerome, and Sedona; and the highest point in the state, Mount Humphreys, in the San Francisco Peaks north of Flagstaff. The third system, Plateau, extends north from the Mogollon Rim—itself a sheer cliff face that reaches heights of 2,000 feet and stretches a third of the way across the state—to cover northern Arizona. Named the Colorado Plateau, this geological region is shared by Arizona's fellow Four Corner states (Colorado, New Mexico, and Utah). It encompasses a series of vast plateaus and deep canyons, the largest and most magnificent of which is the Grand Canyon.

Geographically speaking, Arizona is all over the map, and it's the drastic changes in elevation—from 100 feet above sea level to better than 12,500—that allows for this variety. *Arizona Highways* published an article and photo essay in December 2002 called "A Land for All." It accurately matched landscape shots in Arizona with "twin scenes" in each of the other 49 states, from Vermont to Hawaii and everywhere in between. It has often been said that to drive from Phoenix to Flagstaff is the equivalent of driving from Mexico to Canada: 1,500 miles. And it can all be found within 114,000-plus square miles of what people have come to know as the "desert."

EARLY PEOPLE

The earliest settlers arrived in Arizona somewhere between 20,000 and 40,000 years ago. Back then the state was cooler and wetter, and large game like mammoth wandered the region. These Paleo-Indians, as they are called, were hunters and gatherers who left behind petroglyphs and arrowheads to mark their passage. From the Paleo-Indians evolved perhaps the most interesting of central Arizona's earliest inhabitants, the Hohokam—a Pima Indian word meaning "those who have gone."

The Hohokam (pronounced *hoho-KAM*), who settled in the Salt River Valley several hundred years B.C., started out in small farming groups. Eventually the number of inhabitants expanded into the thousands; by then

Today many of these petroglyphs are easy to see across the state, including at the Deer Valley Rock Art Center in the northwest Valley. (See "Glendale and the West Valley.")

Salado cliff dwellings (or Lower Cliff Dwelling) above Roosevelt Lake at Tonto National Monument

the Hohokam had developed hundreds of miles of canals to support their farms. In the early part of the 15th century, for reasons unknown, the Hohokam and various descendants who had settled in surrounding areas—the Salado to the east and the Sinagua to the north—mysteriously disappeared. Whether it was a long period of drought that hampered their efforts to create life in the desert or a series of economic and political problems, archaeologists cannot agree. But after they left the Valley, their canals fell into disrepair, and the area remained dormant for the better part of four hundred years.

The Hohokam's influence on the area can be seen to this day, in the Native Americans who are considered their descendants as well as in the Salt River Valley, where Phoenix and its neighbors grow and thrive, supported by the original irrigation ditches the Hohokam dug some two thousand years ago.

MODERN NATIVE AMERICANS

The Hohokam, Salado, and Sinagua who had originally farmed the land were gradually replaced by the tribes the Spaniards and Anglos met several hundred years later when they first arrived in central Arizona—the Apache, Yavapai, and Pima Indians.

The Apache are said to have settled into the Southwest about A.D. 1400, slightly overlapping the earlier central Arizona tribes. They were hunter-gatherers who originally saw no need for farming or irrigation. The Yavapai Indians, assumed by many to be the descendants of the earlier Sinagua people, settled in the Verde Valley, and the Pima Indians, who consider themselves descendants of the Hohokam, farmed in the Gila River Valley south of Phoenix.

Today Native Americans represent 19 tribes on 23 reservations—27 percent of the state's 114,000 square miles. The Greater Phoenix area includes the Gila River Indian Community's (www.gilariver.org) 650 square miles south of the city, with 12,000 people, three casinos (Wild Horse Pass, Vee Quiva, and Lone Butte), the Firebird International Raceway, Wild Horse Pass Resort and Spa, and Rawhide Western Town (to name a few).

The Salt River Pima-Maricopa Indian Community (www.srpmic-nsn.gov), meantime, is surrounded by Scottsdale to the west, Fountain Hills on the north, and Mesa to the south.

Many of today's canals were built on the Hohokam's ancient irrigation system

You'll find shops and gas stations along these boundaries selling cigarettes, gas and other goods; the largest shopping center on Native American land in the country, the 140-acre Pavilions on Indian Bend Road west of the Loop 101; two golf courses, Cypress and Talking Stick; and Casino Arizona at McKellips Roads and the recently opened Talking Stick Resort & Casino Arizona at Indian Bend Road, both off the Loop 101. The reservation is also now home to spring training's latest facility, where the Arizona Diamondbacks and Colorado Rockies play in March.

The 40-square-mile Fort McDowell Yavapai Nation (www.ftmcdowell.org) northeast of Phoenix owns the Fort McDowell Casino and the Radisson Fort McDowell Resort & Convention Center.

SOCIAL HISTORY

Theories abound as to how Arizona got its name, including the mispronunciation of an Indian word by Spanish explorers. The Spaniards arrived in the mid-16th century, led by Francisco Vásquez de Coronado on his infamous search for the cities of gold thought to be scattered across the region. What they found instead was desert, which some stories say they aptly named *Arizona,* or "arid zone." For almost three hundred years, the Spaniards swept through Arizona, establishing missions and forts and claiming the area for their monarchy.

Famous missions include San Xavier del Bac in Tucson and Tumacácori near Tubac in southern Arizona.

While Tucson and its southern neighbors served as settlements for the

European newcomers, central Arizona remained largely untouched but for the occasional traveler. After almost three hundred years of Spanish influence, Mexico won its independence in 1821 and quickly clashed with the Americans (in their quest to claim the continent from coast to coast). After the two-year Mexican-American War, the Treaty of Guadalupe Hidalgo was signed, identifying the area as American territory; in 1854 the United States expanded the territory by including what is now the southern strip of Arizona and New Mexico in the Gadsden Purchase.

In 1861, as the rest of the country was entangled in the Civil War, Tucson, the largest settlement at the time, was under constant bombardment from Apache warriors. Without the support of Union soldiers, who had been withdrawn to fight in the East, territorial residents were left to their own devices and voted to form a new territory of the Confederacy. The Confederate government agreed and quickly set up protection. For a short time the region was considered part of the South, until June 1862, when mountain man Kit Carson, along with a regiment of Union soldiers, arrived from California to reclaim the area, making the Battle at Picacho Pass the westernmost conflict of the Civil War. The acquisition led to Arizona becoming its own territory on February 24, 1863.

In response to the Apache raids upon local mines and encampments, the U.S. Army established Fort McDowell on the Verde River, about 18 miles north of the Salt River. The fort and its soldiers needed goods, and suppliers arrived to fill those needs, including John Y. T. Smith, who built the first home in the Valley after

Ocean Trail Bar at Talking Stick Resort

the Hohokam's disappearance, and shortly thereafter Jack Swilling, a shady character and Civil War veteran who fought on both sides of the Mason-Dixon Line. It was Swilling who recognized the value of the irrigation ditches left behind by the Hohokam almost 350 years before; he began cleaning the canals in 1867. Within less than a year the Swilling Irrigation and Canal Company was operational, creating a fertile oasis in the middle of the desert. As settlers arrived, they needed a name for this place they now called home. At the suggestion of self-proclaimed "Lord" Darrell Duppa from England, the Valley was dubbed *Phoenix* after the mythical bird that arose from its own ashes, just as this new town had arisen from the dust of the past.

After the first post office was established in 1869, Phoenix remained a frontier town for quite some time. At the center of the state, far from its sister cities of Tucson, Bisbee, and Tombstone to the south and Prescott and Flagstaff to the north, Phoenix existed unto itself without even a set of railroad tracks passing through. Anything the settlers needed had to be built, invented, or brought in by horse and wagon—a long and tedious journey. The desolation dictated much of life in the late 19th century, influencing everything from area architecture and construction to farming and clothing. Still, the harsh desert encouraged innovation, too.

In 1871, Phoenix was named the seat of Maricopa County; Prescott remained the capital of the territory, as it had been since 1863. As the town grew and new settlers arrived—drawn by the warm weather and the promise of hearty farmland—the canal system expanded. In 1885 the Arizona Canal Company completed the Arizona Canal. This addition became the first expansion beyond the Hohokam's original irrigation system.

In the late 1870s a transcontinental railroad passed through Maricopa, a small town 30 miles to the south of Phoenix, finally providing almost direct access to the area by rail. A stagecoach and freight wagon route carried supplies to and from the station until 1887, when the Maricopa–Phoenix line was completed and opened July 4, finally connecting Phoenix to the rest of the country.

The advent of the railroad significantly influenced Phoenix, introducing new products and creating new opportunities for growth and expansion. In 1889 Phoenix became the territory's capital and home to territorial, federal, and county offices. With the influx of government agencies came a flurry of building as settlers sought to support the growing infrastructure.

While Phoenix offered great opportunity for farmers and their families, opportunities were not equal for all ethnic groups. Native Americans suffered the indignity of curfews and the opening of the Indian School to facilitate the "Americanization" of those under the employ of European landowners. Hispanics and Chinese fleeing discrimination in other regions were relegated to their own communities and religious institutions. Yet from this checkered past Phoenix has risen to host a variety of ethnic groups that celebrate their heritage and history throughout the region.

The desert offered up a number of challenges, but the flexibility and frontier

Roosevelt Dam was completed in 1911

attitude of those who moved to the area for a new life created opportunities. Instead of succumbing to the desert, early residents of the Valley built an infrastructure that would eventually grow to support more than a million people. The summers were hot, and a combination of floods and droughts wreaked havoc on residents and structures alike. Wrestling with Mother Nature in the same battle that the Hohokam eventually abandoned, residents fought the heat and the ebb and flow of water. Relying on their entrepreneurial fervor and desire to survive, they sought new ways to deal with age-old problems. With the creation of the Indian Bend Wash in Scottsdale and dam projects like the Roosevelt Dam at the confluence of the Salt River and Tonto Creek northeast of the city, Valley residents found ways to tame the wild floodwaters that gave the area life—while still keeping enough in reserve to outlast the droughts. Roosevelt Dam was the area's first reliable flood-control system and source of hydroelectric power. The construction of the dam created a 16,000-acre reservoir. A combination of technology and innovation created opportunities for the Valley's new residents and accomplished what the Hohokam could not: control (or at least the appearance of it) over the ebb and flow of water in the Valley—an oasis in the desert.

By the turn of the 20th century, several other agricultural and support communities had established themselves, including Mesa, Tempe, Scottsdale, Glendale, and Peoria; by the end of the first decade, 11,000 people called Phoenix home. On February 14, 1912, Arizona was admitted to the Union as the 48th state and dubbed the Valentine State.

World War I heralded an increased demand for cotton—for uniforms, tires, and airplane fabric—and the Salt River Valley's unique weather created an ideal environment. Farmers changed their fields over to cotton, which became one of the Valley's major commodities and one of Arizona's five c's (cotton, cattle, citrus, copper, and climate). Cotton, coupled with the tire-manufacturing plant in Goodyear, brought more workers; by 1920 the population had almost tripled, making Phoenix the largest city in the state. To accommodate the growing economy, the Southern Pacific Railroad expanded their route to include Phoenix in 1926. Three years later, Phoenix Sky Harbor Airport opened under the ownership of

Scenic Airways, only to be sold shortly thereafter as the Great Depression hit. In 1935 it became the property of the City of Phoenix. As economic downfall swept the nation, the New Deal funded growth statewide, with projects like the 4,500-foot runway for Sky Harbor Airport in Phoenix and Lindley Stadium in Prescott. Such projects lessened the financial burden for many Phoenicians, and the city and its neighbors struggled forward.

Slowly this frontier town began evolving into a full-blown city. Architects designed beautiful homes, the once dusty roads were paved, and in the 1930s the Valley got its name. The Valley of the Sun, as one marketing agency or another began calling Phoenix and its surrounding cities, capitalized on its great weather to promote itself as a tourist spot. About the same time came evaporative coolers (swamp coolers, as they are called by Valley residents today). Gone were the days of sleeping outdoors, and as life became more comfortable for residents, the decision to

Did you know? Once upon a time, the Salt River flowed through the Valley, often flooding its banks and destroying homes and crops. With the building of the Roosevelt Dam, which was dedicated in 1911, the Salt River stopped flowing and created six lakes, including Roosevelt Lake in the Tonto National Forest northeast of the Valley. Today, city bridges cross an often dry riverbed; however, water in Arizona can still wreak havoc, causing bridges to close and roads to wash out.

Fast fact: Arizona will celebrate one hundred years of statehood in 2012.

Cavalliere's Blacksmith Shop, located in Old Town Scottsdale, is a third-generation shop established in 1910

Outrageous Arizona Women

Jana Bommersbach

Pioneering western women were made of stern stuff—they had to be, to face a harsh land where the saloon was the only given, snakes were everywhere, and gunslingers ruled the day. To tame this wild land demanded grit and spit.

Arizona women had these in spades—and with a special twist. Two cultures had already built lives here before the white women joined them, so old Arizona gives us heroines across the color palette.

Here's just a sampling.

There was Lozen, the Apache warrior called "America's greatest guerrilla fighter." She was a prophet, healer, and midwife who fought for her people's freedom for 40 years. She was exiled with Geronimo to a Florida detention camp in 1886 and died in confinement.

There was Pearl Hart of Globe, the only known female stagecoach robber, who pulled off the last stage heist in the Old West in 1899. Eastern media romanticized this pretty "Lady Bandit." Pearl did spend a short time in the Yuma Territorial Prison—inmate #1559—before being mysteriously paroled with a train ticket out of town.

There was Sharlot Hall, the first voice of Arizona literature, the territory's first female officeholder, and the woman who helped cinch Arizona's statehood on Valentine's Day, 1912. A museum in Prescott carries her name and legacy.

There was Luisa Ronstadt Espinel of Tucson, the *first* Ronstadt superstar. This aunt of popular singer Linda Ronstadt was an acclaimed ambassador of culture in the 1920s, performing traditional Spanish and Mexican music throughout the United States and Europe.

Jana Bommersbach is a modern-day outrageous Arizona woman, an acclaimed journalist and author who stands in awe of the women who led the way.

move to the desert became easier. In World War II the desert became a training ground for pilots, and several fields around the Valley opened up, including Luke Air Force Base in the West Valley and Williams Airfield in the East Valley; the area even played host to POWs. Defense contractors—some of which are still here—arrived on the scene, bringing with them more jobs, and even more workers looking for the opportunities the West had become famous for.

By the 1950s, as air-conditioning was introduced, the area's only drawback—its oven-style summers—was suddenly negated, and growth took off. In the 1960s Phoenix acquired more land, bringing its total area to almost 200 square miles, less than half of what it would be some 40 years later. Phoenix and its neighbors expanded outward, growing faster than its highway infrastructure could bear, and drives between outlying areas were long and circuitous, if not impossible. This created a fragmented existence among the cities and prompted immediate plans for expansion, as well as future plans to design and construct ample roads. The implementation of an adequate highway structure has made it easier for the thousands who move here each year. Developers have created several loops around the city, effectively decreasing drive time and connecting Valley cities with the center of Phoenix and one another. As the cities have sprawled outward, developers too often ignored the city centers; recent years, however, have seen these downtown areas return to life. Shops, boutiques, restaurants, wine bars, coffee shops, and parks have flourished, and people have returned to the downtown districts for weekend and evening entertainment.

While the area has grown from agricultural community to metropolitan city, and farmland has given way to subdivisions, Maricopa County is still one of the largest cotton-producing counties in the country. Driving on the highways, you'll see cotton fields interspersed with subdivisions. Still, on the whole, agriculture has given way to service, tourism, and high-tech manufacturing. Cotton remains one of the five *c*'s of the economy, but tourism—precipitated by climate, another of the *c*'s—has grown significantly.

The defense support during World War II has given way to electronics companies, including Motorola, and more than one millionaire has been made. For a while in the 1990s and early 2000s, new homes sprouted seemingly overnight to accommodate the influx of newcomers. Even with 30 percent of residents leaving each month, thousands more arrive, keeping city planners on their toes. The construction boom slowed significantly in 2008 and 2009, and building in the Valley has since leveled out.

In 1995, when Jerry Colangelo (former majority owner of the Phoenix Suns, Arizona Diamondbacks, and Phoenix Mercury) won his bid to bring a baseball expansion team to Arizona, the Arizona Diamondbacks were born. Phoenix became one of the few cities to host all four major-league sports—baseball, football, basketball, and hockey. To welcome their new baseball team, the city built a new ballpark—Bank One Ballpark, renamed Chase Field in 2005 when JP Morgan Chase bought Bank One—in the downtown area, creating new opportunities for expansion and urban infill. Since then the city of Phoenix has set its sights on revitalizing the downtown, as have neighboring Tempe, Gilbert, Chandler, Glendale, Scottsdale, and Mesa.

The Valley will continue to grow as warm weather and the promise of sunshine beckon hordes of people looking for relief from the more severe weather of the East and Midwest. They're swapping bitter winters and the drenching humidity of summer for low humidity, mild winters, and cleaner air—for the most part. Some, unable to stand the heat, will return home, but others will quickly replace them.

The Valley offers year-round enjoyment of the outdoors. In summer, residents have learned to set their clocks a little differently: children bound outdoors after the sun has set, and since Arizona does not observe daylight saving time, the early part of

What are the new five *c*'s?
Arizona Authors and Adventurers—a group of three Arizona travel writers—came up with a new list: cowboys, cacti, chiles, canyons, and casinos.

Fast fact: While Luke Air Force Base is still a working base, Williams Air Force Base in Mesa is now home to Phoenix/Mesa Gateway Airport, which serves commercial passengers.

Fast fact: The D-backs, as they are affectionately called by locals, went on to win the World Series in 2001 against the New York Yankees.

Fast fact: Phoenix still has air-quality advisory days when smog seems to settle in the Valley.

the day becomes a perfect time to run, bike, or golf before the full force of the heat takes effect. Visitors have learned to stay away between May and September, but more and more out-of-town guests have taken to braving the summer for cheaper golf games and deeply discounted resort stays.

Today, 24 towns make up the Phoenix metropolitan area. What was once a series of separate cities and townships has gradually become Greater Phoenix. And while borders may touch, each municipality has retained much of its original charm and individuality—creating a unique experience for those who live here and those who visit.

Transportation

BY HORSE, OF COURSE

Once a way station for travelers on their way to Yuma, California, or Tucson, Phoenix has become a central hub for those seeking the sun. After the Hohokam disappeared from the Salt River Valley in the mid-15th century, the area remained deserted until the late 19th century when a single soldier, astride his horse, rode into the Valley. From then until now, Phoenix has grown steadily; most recently it has grown in leaps and bounds. Cities that once took days to visit are now minutes away, their borders meeting and in some cases melding, the far reaches expanding beyond anything earlier residents ever could have imagined. Those who have lived here less than five years can attest to the fact that this Valley is not the same one they moved to. An intricate highway system, including a series of highway loops, have connected the East Valley with the West, and central Phoenix is now less than an hour to an hour and a half drive (in most cases less than half that) from anywhere in the Valley of the Sun.

> **Did you know?** Arizona does not participate in daylight saving time. During winter and spring Arizona is on Mountain standard time; the rest of the year, Pacific standard time.

GETTING TO PHOENIX

Phoenix is intersected by I-10 and I-17; I-8 passes about 45 miles south of Phoenix near Casa Grande. The area is fairly accessible by car, plane, and bus. The passenger train still doesn't quite make it into Phoenix; AMTRAK stops 30 miles south in the town of Maricopa.

By Bus

Greyhound Lines, Inc., serves Phoenix directly; the local number is 602-389-4200. The station, located at 2115 E. Buckeye Road, is open 24 hours daily, including holidays. There is also a station in Mesa (480-834-3360; 1423 S. Country Club,

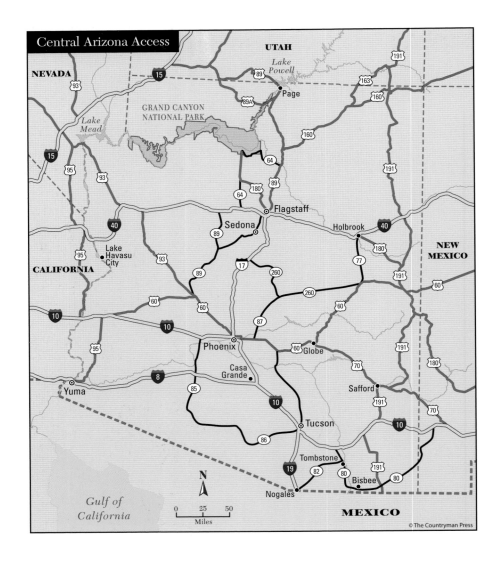

Central Arizona Access

© The Countryman Press

Suite 7), which is open daily. For more information about fares, discounts, and schedules, or to book travel, visit www.greyhound.com, or call the local number for your city.

By Plane

Phoenix is home to one of the 10 busiest airports in the country, with more than 100,000 people coming and going every day. A trip that once meant months of harsh conditions now takes less than a day—and that includes moving through airport security and waiting on late arrivals. Phoenix Sky Harbor International Airport (www.skyharbor.com), which originally opened in 1935, is served by 18 domestic and international airlines, providing nonstop service to more than 100 cities in the United States and worldwide.

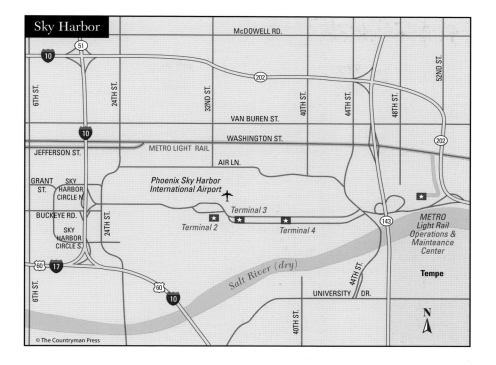

Located 5 miles from downtown Phoenix and easily accessible from the rest of the Valley, Sky Harbor serves as the hub for Tempe-based US Airways (formerly America West) and an operational center for Southwest Airlines. The airport conveniently connects Phoenix and its neighbors to most major domestic cities.

The airport is easily navigable, and renting a car is easy with the 140-acre Rental Car Center, which houses all rental car companies under one roof. Shuttles are available at regular intervals—offering connections to both on- and off-site parking, the Rental Car Center, and many of the local hotels and resorts. Super Shuttle (602-244-9000 or 800-258-3826; www.super shuttle.com) offers service to many locations in the Valley, and you can pick up the Arizona Shuttle at any of the airport's three terminals—2, 3, and 4—to Tucson.

Airlines that Fly to Phoenix

- AeroMexico
- Air Canada
- AirTran
- Alaska Airlines
- Allegiant Air (serves Phoenix-Mesa Gateway Airport)
- American
- British Airways
- Continental
- Delta
- Frontier
- Great Lakes
- Hawaiian Airlines
- JetBlue Airways
- Midwest Airlines
- Southwest Airlines
- Sun Country
- United Airlines
- US Airways
- WestJet

The Other Phoenix Airport

Allegiant Air is making it easier than ever to fly direct to the Phoenix-Mesa area from a number of small cities throughout the Midwest and Oregon and Washington state. For people living in smaller cities, like Sioux Falls, South Dakota, and Peoria, Illinois, getting to an airport with flights to Phoenix can be quite a hassle: troublesome departure times, two- to three-hour drives, and parking fees. Allegiant offers nonstop flights from more than 20 cities to a small handful of popular destinations, including Greater Phoenix.

Allegiant Air flies into **Phoenix-Mesa Gateway Airport** (www.phxmesagate way.org; 6033 S. Sossaman Road), located about 30 miles from Phoenix in the city of Mesa, east of Power Road and south of Ray Road. It's fairly easy to get there using the Loop 202 and/or Highway 60, depending upon where you're driving from/to. You can get directions to the airport and its terminals online. Click on "Flights" on the airport's Web site for a list of cities with service to Phoenix-Mesa; for more about Allegiant Air, visit online at www.allegiantair.com.

By Shuttle

You can also take a shuttle bus to/from Tucson and Flagstaff to the Phoenix airport. Arizona Shuttle (Tucson: 520-795-6771, ext. 118 or Flagstaff: 928-226-8060; www.arizonashuttle.com) picks up every hour at three locations in Tucson and various sites in Flagstaff, and drops off at Terminals 2, 3, and 4 at Phoenix Sky Harbor International Airport several times daily. The Sedona-Phoenix Shuttle (928-282-2068; www.sedona-phoenix-shuttle.com) offers several trips daily to and from Sky Harbor International Airport.

By Train

AMTRAK does not directly service Phoenix by train; however, the AMTRAK Connecting Thruway bus service connects three Phoenix locations with the Maricopa AMTRAK train station 30 miles south of Phoenix. These thruway bus stations are located at the Greyhound station at 2115 E. Buckeye Road; the Phoenix airport at 3400 E. Sky Harbor Boulevard; and the Phoenix-Metro Transition Station at 9617 N. Metro Parkway in north Phoenix. For information about AMTRAK's routes, schedules, and fares, visit www.amtrak.com or call 800-USA-RAIL.

GETTING AROUND THE VALLEY

By Bicycle

With more than 1,345 miles of bike lanes, the Valley is a great place to tour on two wheels. For more information about bicycling here, see the *Outdoor Adventures* sections in each chapter.

Fast fact: There are several other train stations throughout Arizona, including Tucson and Flagstaff.

By Bus

Valley Metro (www.valleymetro.org)—the regional transportation—provides bus service to 12 communities and

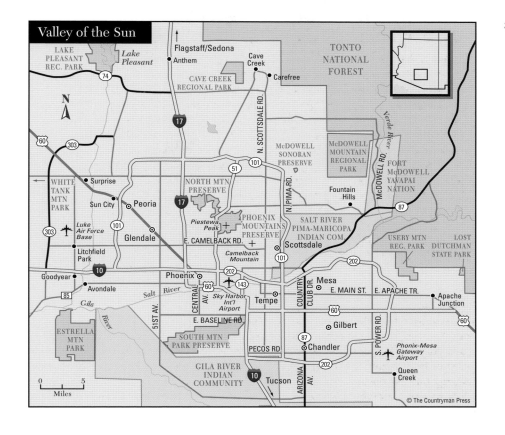

Valley of the Sun

LAKE PLEASANT REC. PARK

Lake Pleasant

74

Flagstaff/Sedona
Anthem

Cave Creek

TONTO NATIONAL FOREST

CAVE CREEK REGIONAL PARK

Carefree

N

60

303

17

N. SCOTTSDALE RD.

51

101

McDOWELL SONORAN PRESERVE

McDOWELL MOUNTAIN REGIONAL PARK

Verde River

McDOWELL RD.

FORT McDOWELL YAVAPAI NATION

Surprise

WHITE TANK MTN PARK

Sun City

Peoria

NORTH MTN PRESERVE

17

N. PIMA RD.

Fountain Hills

303

Luke Air Force Base

101

Glendale

Piestewa Peak

PHOENIX MOUNTAINS PRESERVE

E. CAMELBACK RD.

SALT RIVER PIMA-MARICOPA INDIAN COM.

Scottsdale

87

USERY MTN REG. PARK

LOST DUTCHMAN STATE PARK

Litchfield Park

Camelback Mountain

101

Goodyear

10

202

Mesa

202

Phoenix

60

143

E. MAIN ST.

E. APACHE TR.

Apache Junction

85

Avondale

Salt River

51ST AV.

CENTRAL AV.

Sky Harbor Int'l Airport

Tempe

COUNTRY CLUB DR.

60

60

Gila River

ESTRELLA MTN PARK

E. BASELINE RD.

SOUTH MTN PARK PRESERVE

Gilbert

S. POWER RD.

Phonix-Mesa Gateway Airport

87

PECOS RD.

Chandler

202

Queen Creek

0 5
Miles

GILA RIVER INDIAN COMMUNITY

ARIZONA AV.

10

Tucson

© The Countryman Press

Biking is a great way to get around the Valley of the Sun

works seamlessly with the light rail system. Both the bus and light rail use the same fare system.

With plenty of bike lanes, and buses and light rail trains equipped with bike racks, catching a ride on the bus can quickly take riders to the far-reaching areas of the Valley. For more information about commuting via bike, visit www.azbikeped.org or visit the Valley Metro site for tips on busing with a bike.

Quick tip: Use Valley Metro's online Transit Trip Planner www .valleymetro.org) to map out your route. Plan your trip by departure time or arrival time and get suggested itineraries (including bus and light rail transfers, departure and arrival times, walking distances, directions, and the cost of fare).

By Car

The Valley has a fairly comprehensive highway and interstate system that connects all regions with one another as well as downtown Phoenix. Depending on where you're going and if you're traveling during rush hour (6–9 AM and 3–7 PM), it can take you one and a half hours to get to the outlying areas from Phoenix or vice versa. As you might expect, drivers tend to head toward the city in the morning and away from it during the evening commute; traffic headed in the opposite directions during this time tends to be much lighter. If you're traveling with others, on motorcycle, or have an alternate-fuel vehicle, consider driving in the HOV or high-occupancy vehicle lane (denoted by diamonds) during these peak times. Speed limits within the Valley are 55 and 65 mph.

Note that while most of the permanent highway speed cameras have been decommissioned across the Valley, that may change, and there may still be mobile units that snap pictures of speeding vehicles. Also, note that many intersections throughout the Valley have red-light-running cameras as well as speeding cameras, and several cities host their own mobile units (like Mesa and Tempe), often through school zones.

Keep in mind where your exits are: traversing several lanes of traffic quickly can be difficult for the faint of heart. The following are some tips and descriptions about our local highways and interstates, along with the names they're most commonly known by. If you're listening to any of the local radio stations, you'll often hear their names rather than their numbers.

I-10

Also known as Papago Freeway west of I-17, Maricopa Freeway east of the I-17 interchange, and "the 10," I-10, the main thoroughfare through the heart of the Valley, has an east–west orientation (since it travels most of the country this way). Once it reaches the western outskirts of Tucson to the south, however, it makes a sharp turn north (note that the signage still says EAST and WEST) and travels to Phoenix in a general north–south direction as it passes Sun Lakes, Chandler, Ahwatukee, and Tempe before jogging briefly to the west at the Broadway Curve and passing south of Sky Harbor International Airport before a brief jaunt north again between 16th and 24th streets. At the start of AZ 51 (which heads straight north), I-10 curves sharply to the west, where it passes north of downtown Phoenix, and through Tolleson, Avondale, Goodyear, Litchfield, and Buckeye on its way to Los Angeles.

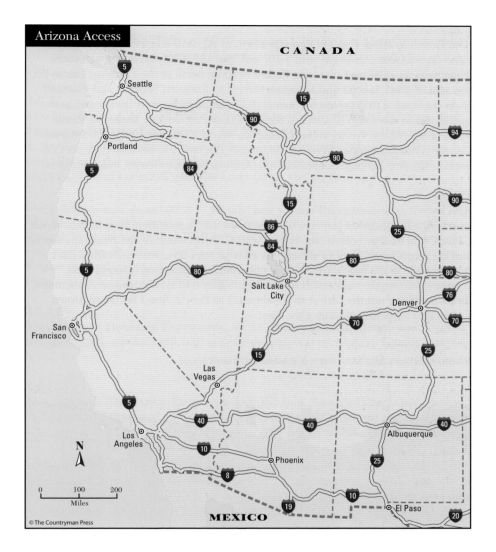

Arizona Access

CANADA

Seattle

Portland

San Francisco

Los Angeles

Las Vegas

Salt Lake City

Denver

Albuquerque

Phoenix

El Paso

MEXICO

N

0   100   200
Miles

© The Countryman Press

I-10 crosses I-17 twice in central Phoenix (together they create a loop around the downtown area)—once by the airport, where I-10 jogs north, and again to the west of downtown Phoenix at the major interchange known locally as the stack, a series of interchanges about 0.5 mile south of McDowell Road by 23rd Avenue.

If you're headed for sites north of the downtown area, I-10 is often your best bet: getting off at Seventh Street or Seventh Avenue (or even the Third Street HOV exit when appropriate) can take you to the Phoenix Art Museum, the Heard Museum, and the Phoenix Public Library (which is actually located at Margaret T. Hance Park—Deck Park, as it's known locally—between Third Street and Third Avenue and situated over the aptly named Deck Park Tunnel).

Car Rental

Travelers arriving via plane can easily rent vehicles at the new Airport Rental Car Center (602-683-3741; 1805 E. Sky Harbor Circle north) at Phoenix Sky Harbor International Airport. The center, conveniently accessible by shuttle, is home to 11 car rental companies. Not all of the rental car companies have counters on-site, but you can pick up their van

Airport Rental Car Center

Company	Toll-Free	Local
Advantage	800-777-5500	602-244-0450
Alamo	800-462-5266	602-244-0897
Avis	800-331-1212	602-261-5900
Budget	800-527-7000	602-261-5950
Dollar	800-800-4000	602-275-0011
Enterprise	800-736-8222	602-225-0588
Fox	800-225-4369	602-252-4399
Hertz	800-654-3131	602-267-8822
National	800-227-7368	602-275-4771
Payless	800-729-5377	602-681-9589
Thrifty	800-847-4389	602-244-0311

service from the center. The multicolored Rental Car Shuttle picks up at the airport curb at the baggage claim level. To return your vehicle from I-10 East, use exit 148, Washington/Jefferson Street. Continue south or straight along the frontage road to Sky Harbor Circle north and turn right. Follow the signs to the lot. If you're traveling from I-10 West, use exit 149, Buckeye Road, and turn left onto Buckeye. Take this road to Sky Harbor Circle south and turn left. Follow the signs. If you're at the airport, simply follow the RENTAL CAR CENTER signs.

By Foot

Areas in the Valley best seen on foot include downtown Phoenix, Mill Avenue and ASU's Tempe campus in Tempe, and downtown or "Old Town" Scottsdale. Other fun walks include downtown Gilbert, downtown Chandler, Mesa's Main Street, and Historic Downtown Glendale. These downtown areas boast local boutiques and restaurants, and many have historic buildings, like the Hotel San Carlos in Phoenix and Crowne Plaza San Marcos Golf Resort in Chandler. Several areas, including Mill Avenue in Tempe and downtown Phoenix, are easily accessible by light rail.

By Light Rail

On December 27, 2008, the first 20 miles of the METRO Light Rail (www.valley metro.org/metro_light_rail) opened to the public, and more than 200,000 people rode the light rail that first weekend. In 2009, more than 11 million riders used the light rail, and in 2010 light rail ridership reached record numbers.

The light rail runs very early morning until midnight during the week; on weekends, the last train arrives at the end of the line at 3 AM. Trains run at 10-minute intervals on

Quick tip: You can take the airport shuttle to the METRO Light Rail station near Sky Harbor Airport. From Arrivals (baggage claim area) leave via the north side exit and cross the street to the center median. Look for the bus marked LIGHT RAIL and hop on for a free ride to the light rail station.

METRO Light Rail

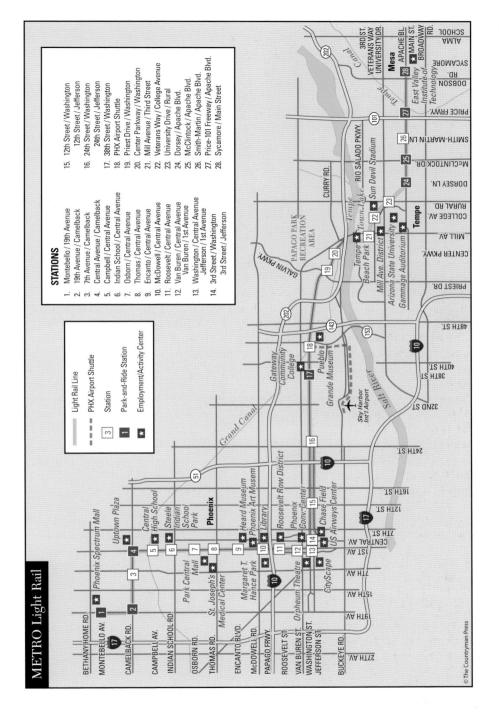

STATIONS

1. Montebello / 19th Avenue
2. 19th Avenue / Camelback
3. 7th Avenue / Camelback
4. Central Avenue / Camelback
5. Campbell / Central Avenue
6. Indian School / Central Avenue
7. Osborn / Central Avenue
8. Thomas / Central Avenue
9. Encanto / Central Avenue
10. McDowell / Central Avenue
11. Roosevelt / Central Avenue
12. Van Buren / Central Avenue
    Van Buren / 1st Avenue
13. Washington / Central Avenue
    Jefferson / 1st Avenue
14. 3rd Street / Washington
    3rd Street / Jefferson
15. 12th Street / Washington
    12th Street / Jefferson
16. 24th Street / Washington
    24th Street / Jefferson
17. 38th Street / Washington
18. PHX Airport Shuttle
19. Priest Drive / Washington
20. Center Parkway / Washington
21. Mill Avenue / Third Street
22. Veterans Way / College Avenue
23. University Drive / Rural
24. Dorsey / Apache Blvd.
25. McClintock / Apache Blvd.
26. Smith-Martin / Apache Blvd.
27. Price-101 Freeway / Apache Blvd.
28. Sycamore / Main Street

Light Rail Line
PHX Airport Shuttle
Station
Park-and-Ride Station
Employment/Activity Center

© The Countryman Press

METRO Light Rail station, downtown Phoenix

weekdays during workday hours, 15-minute intervals on weekends during the day, and 20-minute intervals on Sunday and all other time frames. End to end, the ride takes about 65 minutes, and along the way you have access to a number of Valley hot spots.

You can buy tickets at the kiosks you'll find at every station. To buy multiday passes, visit online: http://fare .app1.valleymetro.org. If you plan to get on and off more than once, buy the all-day pass, which will give you unlimited access for less money.

By Taxi

The Valley is most definitely a car area. Its only system of public transportation is the METRO Light Rail and Bus system. Since most Valley residents must drive to get around, taxis are not usually used; those you will find are most often either at the airport or in front of hotels ready to assist tourists. To get one, you'll need to call one of the 24-hour cab companies.

Did you know? The public art you see at stations along the light rail route as well as certain structural elements of the station itself were the effort of 28 artists from across the United States, in collaboration with light rail engineers, architects, and environmental experts.

While you wait for your train, notice the design elements in the seating, overhead canopies, sidewalks, and so on, as well as the landmarks these artists created to help make the light rail an urban statement.

Quick tip: Bring your bike. The light rail and buses are fully equipped to store your bike. For more about bike etiquette on the light rail, click on the "Bike on Bus" section of the "How to Ride" link at www .valleymetro.org.

Fast fact: There are discount rates for children and seniors.

Mill Avenue light rail station, Tempe

The 20-mile stretch of light rail runs from Sycamore and Main in Mesa to 19th Avenue and Montebello in Phoenix, and it passes a number of well-known sites along the way.

Destination	Station
Tempe Town Lake/Beach Park	Mill Avenue/Third Street
ASU/Sun Devil Stadium	Veterans Way/College Avenue
Sky Harbor Airport	44th Street/Washington Street
Downtown Phoenix/Civic Space Park	Van Buren/Central and First avenues
Phoenix Convention Center	Third Street/Washington and Jefferson streets
Chase Field/US Airways Center	Third Street/Washington and Jefferson streets
Heritage Square/Arizona Science Center	Third Street/Washington and Jefferson streets
Roosevelt District/First Friday	Roosevelt/Central Avenue
Phoenix Art Museum	McDowell/Central Avenue
Heard Museum	Encanto/Central Avenue
Christown Spectrum Mall	Montebello/19th Avenue

NEIGHBORS ALL AROUND

Phoenix is accessible via I-10, I-17, AZ 51, and Loop 101.

Scottsdale is easily accessible from the Loop 101 and Loop 202.

East Valley cities are accessible via I-10, Loop 101, Loop 202, and US 60.

West Valley cities are accessible via I-10, I-17, Loop 101, and Loop 303.

Sedona is approximately 115 miles from Phoenix and accessible from I-17 North. For more detailed information about traveling to and visiting Sedona, see "Sedona."

Phoenix

IN THE VALLEY OF THE SUN

Phoenix and the Valley of the Sun is the largest metropolitan area within Maricopa County's 9,000-plus square miles of Sonoran Desert. Greater Phoenix encompasses 2,000 square miles of rugged, desert terrain; almost 3.8 million people; more than 200 golf courses; professional sports; major sporting events; hundreds and hundreds of restaurants, shops, and boutiques; and a thriving arts and cultural scene. At an elevation of 1,117 feet, Phoenix has an average temperature of 85 degrees and an average rainfall of 7.66 inches a year; it sees more than 300 days of sun annually. It is no wonder that 13 million people visit the Valley each year.

Greater Phoenix is made up of several regions—the city of Phoenix, the East Valley, and the West Valley. Phoenix itself is broken into central Phoenix—comprising downtown, uptown, Phoenix Sky Harbor International Airport, and Papago Buttes; south Phoenix and Ahwatukee, located in the shadows of the Phoenix South Mountain Preserve; and north Phoenix, which extends north past the Loop 101 and includes Piestewa Peak, the Phoenix Mountains, North Mountain, and Shaw Butte.

The city of Phoenix is the fifth largest in the United States, with nearly a million and a half people. It is roughly 515 square miles and extends from about Chandler Boulevard in Ahwatukee on its southern boundary to Jomax Road on the north. It shares its western borders with Glendale, Goodyear, and Avondale; its eastern with Scottsdale and Tempe. Paradise Valley borders Scottsdale and north Phoenix.

Pick Your Spot

Best places to stay in Phoenix, and what you'll find nearby . . .

DOWNTOWN PHOENIX

Downtown Phoenix has its share of high-rises, shadowed sidewalks, and dirty streets, and on game days—the Phoenix Suns (NBA) and Arizona Diamondbacks (MLB) both play down here—and big convention days you can almost believe it's always teeming with energy. On such days, musicians play street side, crowds of people surge along the sidewalks, and the tolling bells of St. Mary's Basilica can barely be heard above

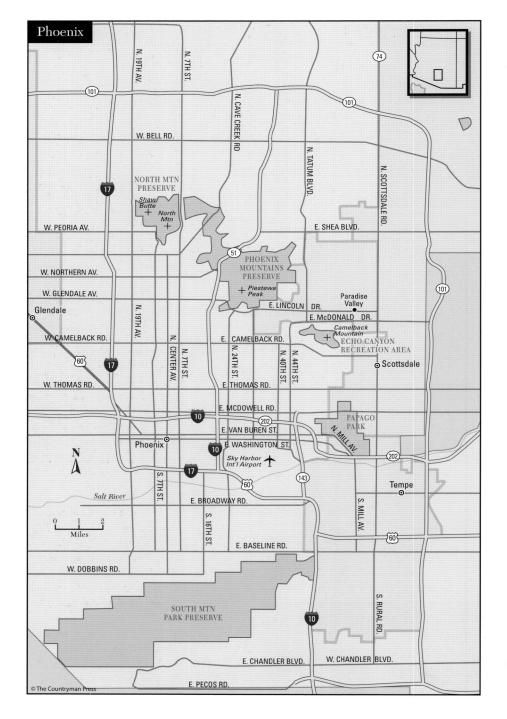

Phoenix

Downtown Phoenix

N

0   0.25
Miles

N. 19TH AV.
N. 17TH AV.
N. 16TH AV.
N. 15TH AV.
N. 13TH AV.
N. 11TH AV.
N. 9TH AV.
N. 7TH AV.
N. 5TH AV.
N. 3RD AV.
N. 1ST AV.
N. CENTRAL AV.
METRO LIGHT RAIL
N. 3RD ST.
N. 7TH ST.

W. ENCANTO BL.

MONTEREY PARK

W. PALM LN.

W. McDOWELL RD.
E. McDOWELL RD.

MARGARET T. HANCE PARK

Burton Barr Central Library

W. CULVER ST.

GRAND AV.
PAPAGO FRWY.
10
10

W. ROOSEVELT ST.
E. ROOSEVELT ST.

Japanese Friendship Garden

N. 1ST ST.
N. 2ND ST.
N. 5TH ST.
N. 9TH ST.

W. McKINLEY ST.

Roosevelt Historic District

W. FILLMORE ST.

UNIVERSITY PARK

Civic Space Park

ASU Downtown

Arizona Center

Children's Museum of Phoenix

W. VAN BUREN ST.

W. MONROE ST.
City Hall
Herberger Theater
St. Mary's Basilica

W. ADAMS ST.
Dodge Theatre

State Capitol

BOLIN MEMORIAL PLAZA

CARNEGIE LIBRARY PARK

W. WASHINGTON ST.
Symphony Hall
Arizona Science Center

W. JEFFERSON ST.
Orpheum Theater
Phoenix Convention Center

S. 19TH AV.
S. 17TH AV.
S. 15TH AV.
S. 9TH AV.
S. 7TH AV.
S. 3RD AV.
S. 1ST AV.
S. CENTRAL AV.
S. 1ST ST.
S. 2ND ST.
S. 3RD ST.
S. 7TH ST.

W. JACKSON ST.
CityScape

US Airways Center

METRO LIGHT RAIL

Chase Field

W. LINCOLN ST.
W. LINCOLN ST.
E. LINCOLN ST.

W. GRANT ST.
W. GRANT ST.
E. GRANT ST.

© The Countryman Press

the din. But other days it's a relaxed and quiet place that offers an excellent opportunity to hit all of the downtown hot spots without any crazy crowds.

Downtown is at the very heart of the city, with CityScape's and Arizona Center's urban shopping, dining, and entertainment venues; several theaters, like the Dodge, Herberger, and Orpheum; Heritage & Science Park (Arizona Science Center, Historic Heritage Square, the Rosson House Museum, and Pizzeria Bianco); sports venues (Chase Field and US Airways Center); and countless restaurants, bars, and shops sprinkled along the one-way streets.

Here you will find the Hyatt Regency Phoenix (800-233-1234; www.phoenix .hyatt.com), which offers front-door access to the Phoenix Convention Center (across the street). The hotel features 712 guest rooms and suites. You'll also find the state's only revolving rooftop restaurant (Compass Restaurant), as well as three additional dining options, a pool, salon, and fitness facility.

Downtown's newest addition to the hotel scene is Sheraton Phoenix Downtown Hotel (800-325-3535; www.sheraton.com). Built in response to the thousands of conventiongoers that flock to downtown Phoenix every year, the Sheraton

The lobby at Sheraton Phoenix Downtown

Phoenix Downtown opened in fall of 2008 as the largest hotel in Arizona with one thousand guest rooms; an on-site coffee bar, restaurant (the District), and bar; as well as a 6,500-square-foot fitness center, spa, and pool.

The historic Hotel San Carlos (866-253-4121; www.hotelsancarlos.com) is a member of the Historic Hotels of America. Built in 1927, Hotel San Carlos was considered one of the most luxurious hotels in the Southwest; it featured air-conditioning and elevators, and beckoned some of Hollywood's most famous stars. In 1955 a swimming pool was added to the third-floor sundeck, and a recent million-dollar renovation has brought the hotel into the 21st century, complete with complimentary wireless Internet access. The hotel offers 121 guest rooms, including 12 suites (rooms are fairly small); you'll also find two restaurants, two bars, a barbershop, and a shoe shine on-site.

The Wyndham Phoenix Hotel (800-359-7253; www.wyndhamphx.com) is on Adams just east of Central and features 532 guest rooms and suites, complimentary Internet access, a swimming pool, and a fitness facility. It offers a full-service concierge service as well as an on-site restaurant and bar and room service.

In midtown Phoenix, where you'll find the Phoenix Art Museum, Heard Museum, and several trendy little restaurants and shops, is the Clarendon Hotel (602-252-7363; www.goclarendon.com), made famous in 1976 as the location of the alleged mob hit on *Arizona Republic* journalist Don Bolles. The hotel has made quite a name for itself in recent years as a boutique hotel with friendly service and great space. It's made more than its fair share of top travel lists among *Travel + Leisure* magazine and the Travel Channel, and it is most notable for its rooftop deck and lounge (check out these incredible views day or night), and the Oasis, its on-site pool that's part water feature, part pool and a little bit of heaven.

Off I-10 near the Phoenix-Tempe border is Arizona Grand Resort (866-267-1321; www.arizonagrandresort.com). Located at the base of the Phoenix South Mountain Preserve, this 200-acre property features six on-site restaurants, including a poolside bar and grill; spa and athletic club; 740 rooms; and an 18-hole golf course. It's close to 60 miles of hiking trails and easily accessible from I-10. The resort is child-friendly, featuring a 7-acre water park and supervised children's activities. It makes a great escape during the hotter seasons; locals love the summer packages.

NORTH PHOENIX: I-17/BLACK CANYON FREEWAY

This commerce corridor is located in northwest Phoenix and offers easy access to West Valley cities, including Glendale, Sun City, Peoria, and Surprise. Area attractions include University of Phoenix Cardinals Stadium, Glendale Arena, Lake Pleasant, and Arrowhead Towne Center. Hotels include the 250-room Crowne Plaza Phoenix (888-797-9878; www.cpphoenix.com), with amenities like earplugs, eye mask, lavender spray, and a sleep CD. You'll also find free Internet access, a complimentary shuttle within a 5-mile radius, express check-in and checkout, and an on-site restaurant and bar. There's also the 284-room Four Points Sheraton Phoenix Metrocenter (602-997-5900; www.starwoodhotels.com/fourpoints), located close to the Metrocenter Mall; it has free wireless Internet access, pool and spa, and an on-site restaurant and bar.

Farther north (north of the Loop 101) and east of I-17 is the JW Marriott Desert Ridge Resort & Spa (800-898-4527; www.jwdesertridgeresort.com). The sprawling resort covers 316 acres and has 10 distinct dining experiences, championship golf, and the Revive Spa. At night it looks like a desert mirage. The grounds are meticulously kept, the staircases are sweeping and grand, and the ceilings are vaulted. There are 950 guest rooms and 81 suites. The resort is close to shopping at Desert Ridge Marketplace and Kierland Commons as well as hiking at Pinnacle Peak.

Pointe Hilton Squaw Peak Resort (800-876-4683; www.pointehilton.com) is a family-friendly resort in north Phoenix. Its Hole-in-the-Wall River Ranch, on-site spa and salon services, and nearby golf, hiking, and shopping choices offer options for a variety of tastes. Conveniently located in north-central Phoenix off Piestewa Peak Parkway (formerly Squaw Peak Parkway), this Pointe Hilton resort, surrounded by beautiful mountain views, features spacious two-room suites and one- and two-bedroom casitas. Complimentary high-speed Internet access; child care services and activities. Pets are welcome. Enjoy close proximity to shopping, dining, and golf in the Biltmore District/Camelback Corridor and hiking at Piestewa Peak.

Pointe Hilton Tapatio Cliffs Resort (800-876-4683; www.pointehilton.com) is farther north than the Pointe Hilton Squaw Peak Resort and features an on-site 18-hole golf course as well as a full-service spa and Falls Water Park—a series of pools, waterfalls, and a 130-foot enclosed slide. Babysitting and children's programs are available. The resort features two-room suites, complimentary Internet access, and five on-site dining opportunities, including Cascade Falls—a poolside eatery.

Local Flavors

Taste of the town . . . local
restaurants, cafés, bars, bistros,
etc.

RESTAURANTS

Downtown Phoenix

Downtown Phoenix is home to a number of independent Arizona favorites you won't find anywhere else, including Hanny's (602-252-2285; www.hannys .net), on the southwest corner of Adams and First Street. Hanny's is a fairly new restaurant in a visually recognizable architectural space built in 1947 (that's old for Phoenix). Open at 11 for lunch and dinner (5 on Saturday and Sunday), the kitchen cooks pizzas, salads, and sandwiches until 1 AM daily, which can be a rarity in downtown Phoenix, when much of the area closes evenings and weekends. Not all hotel restaurants are worth mentioning; however, District (602-817-5400; district restaurant.com), officially known as District American Kitchen and Wine Bar located street-level at Sheraton Phoenix Downtown Hotel is an exception. Its menu—comfort food with a sophisticated flair—paired with its urban locale and trendy décor, makes it a unique stop in downtown Phoenix. The District is one of the many Arizona restaurants committed to local growers and sustainable farming and boasts its own garden. (See the "Restaurant Gardens" side bar later in this chapter.) The menu reflects locally-made and -grown goods—like beer made in Sedona and tomatoes from Wilcox.

Just as Majerle's Sports Grill (602-258-0118; www.majerles.com), owned by a famed Phoenix Suns's player, caters to Suns fans, Alice Cooper's-town (602-253-7337; www.alicecoopers town.com), owned by unabashed baseball fan, Phoenix native, and rock star Alice Cooper, caters to D-back fans. The slogan at Alice Cooper'stown—"Where jocks and rock meet"—captures the essence of the legendary musician's gastronomic tribute to music and sports. Located just a short walk from Chase Field and US Airways Center, it's a good place to grab a bite before or after a baseball (or basketball) game.

If you like this . . . you might also try these great locations, just a short walk from Chase Field and/or US Airways Center: Coach & Willie's (602-254-5272; www.coachandwillies.com) and Hard Rock Café (602-261-7625; www.hardrockcafe.com)

For a fun, unique lunch outing, consider Friday's Front Row Sports Grill (602-462-3503; www.frontrow phoenix.com), located at Chase Field overlooking left field and third base. Good food, good drinks, and a *great* view. Ask about patio seating even if there's not a game going on—sometimes you can catch the Arizona Diamondbacks at batting practice. What a relaxing way to spend a spring afternoon! The entrance is located on the north side of Chase Field on Jefferson Street, between Fourth and Fifth streets, Gate L.

Looking for a quick and delicious lunch in downtown Phoenix? Consider Duck and Decanter (602-266-6637;

Quick tip: On game days, reserve a table at Friday's Front Row outside on the patio. Tickets go on sale the first of the month for the next month's games. Tickets for July, for instance, would go on sale June 1. For pricing or to reserve a table, call 602-462-3503.

Quick tip: For more food choices, check out CityScape www.city scape.com) at One East Washington. The multiuse space is downtown Phoenix's newest eating, shopping and entertainment venue, where you'll find a variety of options from Five Guys Burgers and Fries to luxury bowling at Lucky Strike Lanes to shopping at Urban Outfitters.

favorites—makes his own mozzarella, tops each pizza with the freshest ingredients he can find, and bakes it in a wood-fired brick oven (brought back from the Old Country). The lines are long, and reservations are taken for groups of 6–10 only. No take-out, so the only way to experience this very popular pizza place is to wait. And it's worth it!

If you like this . . . try Bar Bianco, adjacent to Pizzeria Bianco, for drinks and appetizers while you wait, or Pane Bianco, on Central north of Indian School, for take-out lunch.

www.duckanddecanter.com). This Valley staple has fed area residents since 1972. On offer are sandwiches, soups, salads, and other goodies, including specialty wines, beers, cheeses, coffees, and teas. The Duck (as it is affectionately called by locals) has some of the best and most inventive sandwiches around, including signature creations like Where's the Beef? (a vegetarian concoction packed with so many tasty ingredients, you forget to ask where the beef is) and The Duckling (smoked breast of duck, smoked turkey, cream cheese, cranberry walnut relish, and watercress on walnut raisin country bread, a meal that confounds your taste buds into a state of stunned joy). The Duck's three locations are favorites of the city's lunchtime crowd, so expect to wait in line—but it's worth it. You can call ahead or order online for faster pickup.

It seems that Bronx native Chris Bianco has single-handedly put Phoenix on the pizza map with his world-renowned Pizzeria Bianco (602-258-8300; www.pizzeriabianco.com). Considered by some to have the best pizza the world over, Bianco—winner of the James Beard Best Chef: Southwest award, and Phoenix proprietor of not one, not two, but three local

For a taste of the Southwest in all of its mixed-up glory, try Sam's Café (602-252-3545; www.canyoncafe.com) at the Arizona Center. This upscale restaurant is worth a visit. Its two locations in the Valley serve Nuevo Southwestern fare that is simply delicious. Traditional dishes like meat loaf, pasta, and mashed potatoes have been infused with a mixture of Mexican, Native American, and western U.S. flavors, creating dishes like pasta with a jalapeño cream sauce; meat loaf stuffed with peppers, bacon, and onions, topped with roasted tomato barbecue sauce; and mashed potatoes blended with green chiles. They also serve chimichangas, fajitas, and enchiladas. Their margaritas are top-notch—try the Grand Canyon, a house margarita that's a mixture of cranberry, lime, and

Fast fact: Pizzeria Bianco is located at Heritage & Science Park, off Seventh Street between Monroe and Jefferson.

Fast fact: There's a Sam's Café at Biltmore Fashion Park on Camelback Road.

Quick tip: If you're not into crowds, you may want to avoid downtown Phoenix and the Roosevelt Row District on First Fridays (an art walk to the nth degree); it can be fairly overwhelming if you're new in town or just visiting. However, if you're really into catching the Phoenix art scene, the first Friday of every month is the time to check it out!

orange juice; tequila; and juice from the prickly pear cactus native to the Sonoran Desert. Ask for it on the rocks with salt.

The Roosevelt Row District (www.rooseveltrow.org) is a fairly recent phenomenon. Once a decaying neighborhood on the north edge of downtown Phoenix, Roosevelt Row has evolved into a trendy artist community

Sens, in the Roosevelt Row District

with a variety of restaurants, bars, and art galleries, many of which are converted 1920s bungalows. Among them are Sens Asian Tapas & Sake Bar (602-340-9777; www.sensake.com), a unique little Japanese tapas bar that serves up specialty fare at delicious prices. Designed to entice you to try a little of everything, the menu prices range from $3 to $9 for its appetizer-sized portions. Sens also offers a list of filtered (sweeter) and unfiltered sake choices. Or order a dry martini made with their house-infused vodkas— lychee or lemongrass, to name a few. The restaurant is located on First Street, just south of McKinley and between the Van Buren and Roosevelt light rail stops on Central Avenue.

If you like this . . . try Moira Sushi & Kitchen Bar (602-254-5085; www.moirasushi.com). You'll find fresh sushi and a splash of red and blue lights at this spot located just off Third Street and McKinley (south of Roosevelt).

On North Third Street, a short walk from the light rail, is The Roosevelt Tavern (602-254-2561; www.twitter.com/roosevelttavern), owned by Matt Pool of Matt's Big Breakfast fame. This svelte, cozy little neighborhood bar boasts a beer list that just might outdo its wine list. Pick a place, any place—this converted bungalow's rooms are small, intimate, and candlelit, with wood flooring, black leather furniture, and green walls. Sit at the bar, nab a table for two, or feast with locals at the communal table. To accompany the wine and beer lists is a delightfully playful menu of snacks that range from a beer-steamed hot dog to an artisanal cheese plate. The Roosevelt is located in the middle of the block on Third Street, between McKinley and Garfield (just south of Roosevelt).

If you like this . . . try Carly's Bistro (602-262-2759; www.carlys bistro.com) on Roosevelt, a full restaurant and bar that serves late eats (midnight during the week and 2 AM on weekends), or the Lost Leaf (602-258-0014; www.thelostleaf.org), a tiny bar on Fifth Street just south of Roosevelt; it's open daily 5 PM–2 AM.

Uptown/Midtown Phoenix

Farther north in what is considered uptown and midtown Phoenix is Coronado Café (602-258-5149; www.coronadocafe.com). Located in the historic Coronado District in central Phoenix, this neighborhood favorite is a 1915 Craftsman-style bungalow refurbished into a cozy and inviting dining experience. The Coronado Café offers soups, salads, and sandwiches for lunch, along with a daily special such as chicken enchiladas or baked salmon. The dinner menu includes appetizers, soups, salads, and sandwiches as well as featured entrées—Bing cherry barbecued chicken or oven-roasted Alaskan halibut. Once a BYOB establishment, the café's full-service bar now includes cocktails, specialty drinks, wines by the glass or bottle, and international and regional beer.

If you like this . . . try Coronado Café for weekend brunch, when they break out the eggs for a number of tasty dishes—scrambled, poached, or done up omelet style.

At Durant's (602-264-5967; www.durantsfinefoods.com), you have to enter through the kitchen, unless you want to be pegged as a tourist; in fact, most locals can't even tell you where the front door is! Founded by Jack Durant, this restaurant, located at the corner of Central and Virginia in central Phoenix, continues to boast red velvet and black vinyl decor—the interior is dark and "smoky." You can almost imagine the air thick with cigar smoke, raucous laughter, and big dealings of the 1950s. The food is delicious, the staff friendly, and the clientele respectful of the restaurant's desire to keep itself firmly entrenched in the past. Cell phones are not allowed—in fact, if you stop to chat, you may be asked to leave. Enjoy this treat and take a step into the Old West when John Wayne might have visited. The prices are a bit high, but the journey back makes it worth it!

An authentic Arizona experience, Fry Bread House (602-351-2345), on N. Seventh Avenue, is a must-do while you're in Phoenix. A Native American staple throughout the Southwest, fried bread—or fry bread—is just as delicious as it sounds. Similar to the elephant ears of the midwestern carnival or Mexican sopapillas, it can be eaten plain, salted, or with honey; it's also used like tortillas to make Indian tacos.

My Florist Café (602-254-0333; www.myfloristcafe.com) is located at the corner of Seventh Avenue and McDowell, right in the middle of the Phoenix historic districts. This is a popular choice for breakfast, lunch, dinner, or even a late-evening meal. My Florist Café (named as such because that's what the big sign above it says, and the city of Phoenix would not allow a new one to replace it) features an impressive array of soups, salads, and sandwiches. Breakfast choices include a yogurt and granola parfait, breakfast burrito, and salmon plate. Lunch and dinner include a variety of gourmet sandwiches (including the Portabello—roasted portobello, eggplant, red pepper, and more on a rosemary focaccia bread) and salads like the Brie Salad (Brie, chicken, fresh berries, roasted almonds . . . and the list goes on). The dinner menu adds a number of appetizers, and the bar serves mixed drinks and wine, including several choices by the glass. Enjoy live piano music (Nicole Pesce on the concert grand Steinway) Wednesday–Sunday 7:30 PM–midnight.

Biltmore District/Camelback Corridor
With its numerous four star/five diamond resorts, the Biltmore-Arcadia area of Phoenix (along and south of Camelback Road) features a number of excellent resort-hotel restaurants, including bistro 24 (602-952-2424; www.ritz carlton.com) at the Ritz-Carlton. This American-style bistro, befitting the elegance and sophistication of the Ritz-Carlton, serves a seasonal menu steeped in classical French training and influenced by international cuisine.

El Chorro Restaurant and Lodge (480-948-5170; www.elchorrolodge .com) was originally built in 1934 by John C. Lincoln (you may have seen the hospital named after him) as the Judson School for Girls. Since then, it has had various owners. Most recently it underwent a transformation at the hands of local philanthropist and Paradise Valley resident Jacquie Dorrance in 2009. The 11-acre property features some of the best dining views in the area; an upscale menu for brunch, lunch, and dinner; evening entertainment Wednesday–Saturday; and a game of boccie anytime.

A Valley institution, Havana Café (602-952-1991; www.havanacafe-az.com) has been pleasing guests since 1989. Adapted from traditional Cuban foods and influenced by Spanish and Latin American cuisine, this menu—developed by chef-owner B. J. Hernandez—has created a following of loyal patrons, facilitating the opening of an additional restaurant in Scottsdale. B. J. and her husband, Gilbert, have been racking

up the awards and rave reviews—Best Flan, Best Tapas Bar, Best Black Bean Soup. You'll find combinations of sweet peppers, garlic, and tomatoes; plantains, tropical fruit, and veggies; and traditional Cuban recipes like the Emperadado Cubano. Stop by and try these delectable dishes for yourself.

Over on 16th Street just south of Camelback Road is another Phoenix favorite: Coup des Tartes (602-212-1082; www.nicetartes.com). An ambience of candlelight, bare wooden floors, and French-bistro cuisine has transformed this 1930s farmhouse into a cozy little French restaurant with only 14 tables. Coup des Tartes is the brainchild of chef-owner Natascha Ovando-Karadsheh, a 1996 graduate of the French Culinary Institute in New York City. This little BYOB encourages you to bring your favorite bottle of wine ($8 corkage fees on regular-sized bottles) to complement their ever-changing menu. You will find appetizers like Canadian Cove mussels from Prince Edward Island; an exquisite plate of creamy cheeses, nuts, and fruit both fried and fresh; and the house favorite, Brie Brûlée (warm Brie topped with caramelized apples and served with toast and fruit). Salad options might include a mixture of endives, oranges, walnuts, and dates drizzled with creamy tarragon vinaigrette. Entrées feature filet mignon, lobster, Chilean sea bass, and vegetarian fare crafted into culinary masterpieces. Tarts are baked fresh every day; these mouthwatering once-in-a-lifetime treats are made with real butter.

Other area restaurants include NOCA (602-956-6622; www.restaurant noca.com), short for North of Camelback. Open for dinner Tuesday–Sunday (and Monday December–April), this upscale restaurant features a menu of pasta and seafood, as well as a four-

Quick tip: Reservations recommended on Friday and Saturday nights—though cancellations do occur to accommodate those spur-of-the-moment dinner decisions.

course chef's tasting menu that can be paired with wine from a comprehensive wine list (by the glass, half bottle, or bottle). For something more casual, you can get your burger on at Delux (602-522-2288; www.deluxburger.com). While the menu reflects American favorites (burgers, soups, salads, and apple pie), this is not your local diner. Instead think sophisticated and chic— you might find chocolate milk shakes on the menu, but they're sharing space with orange blossom martinis, micro-brewery beer flights, and a $92 bottle of Veuve Clicquot Yellow Label.

South Phoenix/Airport

In Phoenix near the airport, you'll find the historic Stockyards Restaurant & 1889 Saloon (602-273-7378; www .stockyardsrestaurant.com). The Stock-yards is Arizona's original steakhouse and has served the Valley for more than 50 years. Originally part of the Tovrea Cattle Ranch, the restaurant serves prime rib, hand-cut steaks, and fresh seafood. Steeped in the area's rich ranching culture, the 1889 Saloon features a massive hand-carved cherry-and-mahogany bar and a cut-glass chandelier.

Farther south near the South Mountain Preserve, south Phoenix (or as the locals call it, SoMo—short for South Mountain) is developing a name for itself. Here is where you'll find The Farm at South Mountain (602-243-9081; www.thefarmatsouthmountain .com), closed during the summer months. The property includes a 10-

acre pecan grove with three restaurants in three distinct settings; stalls selling handmade goods, herbs, and plants; and a farmer's market on Saturday that sells great breads from some of the Valley's best bakeries.

One of the farm's eateries, Quiessence (602-276-0601; www .quiessencerestaurant.com), is a charming little restaurant that does its best to support local growers and in the process creates an ever-changing and delightful mix of native flavors. Take your time and enjoy the experience; dinner is a meal to be savored here.

Another farm eatery, Morning Glory Café (602-276-8804), offers a wonderful outdoor dining experience. Sit on the garden patio beneath the mesquite and palo verde trees, and relax for a wonderful breakfast of fresh muffins, scones, freshly squeezed orange juice, or just-brewed coffee; the omelets and breakfast burrito include veggies from the garden. Weekends usually mean a wait, but you can browse the fresh breads, plants, herbs, and handmade goods at the assortment of outdoor stalls.

Lastly, The Farm Kitchen (602-276-7288) is located at the front of The Farm at South Mountain's property and serves breakfast pastries and lunch cafeteria style. Order from the menu inside and relax outside at one of the many picnic tables.

Quick tip: To reach Quiessence, pull into the Farm at South Mountain's rock parking lot and follow the tree-lined drive to another parking lot. Park here; you'll see the lights of the restaurants peeking from among the plants and trees. Follow the footpath through the gardens to the back of the property, where you'll see a sign marking your way.

Restaurant Gardens

Geri Koeppel

Not content to just buy fresh and local, several Valley restaurants also grow their own ingredients on premises or in nearby gardens.

Joe's Farm Grill (480-563-4745; www.joesfarmgrill.com) in Gilbert isn't just a name: owner Joe Johnston's 15-acre farm on the property provides herbs, fruit, and vegetables for a weekly farm market and his retro/futuristic hamburger stand.

LON's at the Hermosa (602-955-7878; www.lons.com) in Paradise Valley grows herbs, melons, eggplant, tomatoes, and greens, among other items, on an acre garden outside the kitchen. Workers in their chef's whites tend plants and harvest the bounty for their gourmet dishes.

The organic garden at **Latilla at the Boulders** (602-579-2631; www.theboulders.com) in scenic Carefree spans more than 5,000 square feet and yields vegetables, citrus, and berries, which are used in dishes such as short ribs with radishes or pomegranate pico de gallo.

At Caffé Boa (480-968-9112; www.cafeboa.com) in Tempe, every staff member is required to put in hours at a community garden in downtown Tempe. Planting began in spring of 2010, and they anticipate growing a cornucopia of vegetables, herbs, and citrus on 0.75 acre.

Even urban restaurants are getting down and dirty. **District at the Sheraton Phoenix Downtown** (602-817-5400; www.districtrestaurant.com) removed ornamental cacti on its fourth-floor deck and planted tomatoes, peppers, lettuce, and herbs. Raised herb and vegetable beds hug the exterior wall of **Parlor Pizzeria** (602-248-2480; www.theparlor.us) in central Camelback; they top pizzas with the aromatic herbs at no charge.

Caffé Boa

Also, at **Quiessence** (602-276-0601; www.quiessencerestaurant.com), Chef Greg LaPrad buys from Maya's Farm, adjacent to his south Phoenix restaurant, and Kai (602-385-5726) sources from growers on the surrounding Gila River Reservation.

Geri Koeppel is a Phoenix-based freelance writer specializing in food and drinks.

West Phoenix
Garcia's Las Avenidas (602-272-5584; www.theoriginalgarcias.com), founded by Julio and Olivia Garcia in west Phoenix back in 1956, went on to become a nationally recognized chain. This restaurant, however, remains within the family that started it all. Good, traditional, inexpensive Mexican foods have kept this a local favorite.

WINE BARS

Downtown Phoenix

Cheuvront Restaurant & Wine Bar
(602-307-0022; www.cheuvronts.com),
on Central Avenue in the north end
of downtown Phoenix, is a city favorite
and has been recognized on the
national stage by *Bon Appétit* as one
of the 50 best restaurants in the United States. The menu offers an array
of dishes to choose from, including
entrées like the maple bourbon glazed
pork chop and pan-seared Alaskan
halibut. Cheuvront rounds out its
menu with eclectic pizzas, tasty gourmet salads, and a variety of cheese
plates designed to delight the senses.
Enjoy the added element of suggested
wine pairings on your menu, or ask
your server to assist you in making a
choice that will heighten your dining
experience. If you're new to wine, sit at
the bar, and the bartender can point
out excellent choices based on your
novice tastes. Hungry? Ask him or her
to pair your wine with a tasty cheese
plate. Oh, and they make an excellent
mojito—perfect for a hot summer
afternoon!

Biltmore District/Camelback Corridor

Sportsman's Fine Wine & Spirits
(602-955-WINE; www.sportsmans
wine.com) has been in the Valley
(under one owner or another) since
the 1950s; the current owners have
been at the helm since 1987 and have
transformed its focus from somewhere
to buy a six-pack to the place where
you can purchase fine wine and spirits.
You'll find single-malt scotch, whiskey,
rum, and other spirits; sparkling and
still wines; and a collection of beers—
all from various points on the globe—
as well as a wine bar, tastings, and
events ranging from a classic malt sem-

Fast fact: Sportsman's is adjacent
to another Valley favorite—Tarbell's
(602-955-8100; www.tarbells.com)
—an intimate, romantic restaurant
with impeccable service, mouthwatering fare, and ultrahigh standards.
(They only serve their peach short-
cake when the peaches are at the
height of their season.)

inar to Irish beer tastings. The wine
bar serves appetizers; a comprehensive
list of cheeses; and sandwiches and salads for lunch and dinner. Check out
the lengthy menu of wines by the glass.

FARMER'S MARKETS

The weekly **Downtown Phoenix Public Market** (www.phoenixpublicmarket
.com) features Arizona agriculture,
cooking, and creativity as vendors from
across the state bring their best to
Phoenix. You will find handmade noo-
dles; olive oil from the Valley's own
Queen Creek Olive Mill; delicious
hummus and pita chips by Dr. Hummus; wines from Granite Creek
Vineyards in Chino Valley north of
Phoenix; fresh eggs, vegetables, and
herbs from local growers; and handmade crafts like necklaces and hand-
bags. Listen to live music and wander
among the shaded stalls on this usually
empty lot.

*If you like this . . . you'll love the
recently opened Phoenix Public Market
at the southeast corner of Central and
McKinley, which sells local favorites all
week long. The little grocery also features local wines (by the glass or bottle), and sandwiches and soups and
coffee bar 'round back.*

48 Hours

If you don't have much time to spend here, or if you've only allocated a couple of days of your vacation to Phoenix, this short-trip itinerary will give you an idea of what to do while you're here.

GETTING THERE

Downtown Phoenix puts you in the heart of the city's arts, sports, and entertainment districts. Located roughly between Seventh Street and Seventh Avenue, north of Lincoln to about Roosevelt Street just south of I-10, downtown Phoenix offers plenty to do, from major league baseball games at Chase Field and NBA basketball at US Airways Center to performing arts at the Herberger, Orpheum, and Dodge theaters and Symphony Hall.

If you like this . . . you might also like the brand new CityScape (www.cityscapephoenix.com) project that opened in the fall of 2010. Located at the corner of First and Washington, the mixed-use urban development offers shopping, dining, and entertainment in the center of downtown.

You'll also find the METRO Light Rail and plenty of stops along its route, from the **Cibo** (602-441-2697; www.cibophoenix.com), a bungalow

Quick tip: For an excellent selection of Arizona maps, hiking and trail guides, and history and travel books about the state, visit locally owned Wide World of Maps (www.maps4u.com). They have three locations in the Valley: Phoenix, Scottsdale and Mesa.

turned urban pizzeria, to Seamus McCafffrey's Irish Pub and Restaurant (602-253-6081; www.seamusmc caffreys.com), on Monroe next to the Hotel San Carlos. The area is spread out over about 2 miles or so of city blocks, but the light rail makes it easy to hop from place to place.

If you're downtown, you'll want to make Pizzeria Bianco (602-258-8300; www.pizzeriabianco.com) your choice for dinner. Chances are there will be a line before it opens at 5 PM, especially if there's a game downtown. No worries, simply find a place at the adjacent Bar Bianco (602-528-3699), which opens an hour earlier, for drinks and appetizers while you wait for your turn to partake in Chris Bianco's heavenly pies.

Post drinks, take your place at Pizzeria Bianco for one of Bianco's world-famous pizza pies. Pizzeria Bianco is perhaps the most famous of Chef Chris Bianco's triumvirate of eateries (Bar Bianco and a sandwich shop, Pane Bianco, round out the trio). It can be found at Heritage & Science Park in downtown Phoenix. Just follow the line! On game nights you'll find impatient guests queued up outside this hip little garage-turned-restaurant (complete with old grease spots on the floor). Bianco, a Bronx native, serves his world-renowned pizza the only way (for New Yorkers)—straight from the brick oven. Winner of the James Beard Best Chef: Southwest award, Bianco has made perfecting the pizza his life-work, and it has not gone unnoticed by locals, tourists, or the world of international foodies. These pies present such ingredients as pistachios and house-made mozzarella or salami, making pizza an art form.

In addition to the numerous bars and clubs that comprise downtown Phoenix, there are also a number of

Quick tip: Heritage & Science Park is located off Seventh Street between Monroe and Jefferson. Your best bet for parking is the garage at Fifth Street and Monroe. Note that Monroe is one-way headed north.

entertainment venues. Consider a play or dance performance at Orpheum Theatre (www.phoenix.gov/convention center/orpheum) or Herberger Theater (602-254-7399; www.herberger theater.org), where Actors Theatre (602-252-8497; www.atphx.org), Arizona Theatre Company (www.az theatreco.org), and the Center Dance Ensemble perform; a live performance by the Phoenix Symphony (602-495-1999 or 800-776-9080; www.phoenix symphony.org); or a concert at Dodge Theatre (602-379-2800; www.live nation.com/venue/dodge-theatre -tickets).

DAY 1

Take a Hike

Work off last night's pizza with a short, intense hike that climbs above the Valley floor. Piestewa Peak's Summit Trailhead—part of Phoenix Mountains Park and Recreation Area/Dreamy Draw Park (602-262-7901)—is located on Squaw Peak Drive off Lincoln Drive between 22nd and 24th streets. This trail is a 2.5-mile round-trip hike that gains more than 1,200 feet in elevation. Its views, which almost rival those of Camelback Mountain, provide hikers with a different perspective of the Valley. Other hiking trails are accessible from the various lots in the park and recreation area and from Dreamy Draw Park.

If you like this . . . but want a longer hike meant for an experienced hiker, try Camelback Mountain along the Phoenix, Scottsdale, and Paradise Valley borders. See the Scottsdale chapter for more info.

Late Breakfast/Early Lunch

You're bound to be hungry after your hike, so make Matt's Big Breakfast (602-254-1074; www.mattsbigbreak fast.com) one of those late breakfast/ early lunch kind of deals (or get in early before your hike—they open at 6:30 AM). Prepare for a bit of a wait at this tiny restaurant (it seats 26 at the most); you can wait outside and enjoy the Phoenix weather. The wait is worth it. Matt Pool and his wife, Erenia Lara, believe in buying only the finest ingredients. This means the delicious bacon comes from the Pork Shop in Queen Creek and the cage-free eggs come from Chino Valley Ranchers in Southern California. The pancakes are made from scratch, and the hash browns are like nothing you've ever tasted before. No matter what you order, you'll be happy with it; unfortunately, you'll have to return to try all of the other goodies on the menu.

Afternoon Sight-Seeing

The Heard Museum (602-252-8848; www.heard.org) was founded in 1929 by Dwight B. and Maie Bartlett Heard to house their personal collection of cultural and fine art. It is now a private, nonprofit museum dedicated to preservation, awareness, and education of Native American culture and art, specifically of the Southwest. The museum includes about 35,000 objects; displays within the 10 exhibit halls and outdoor courtyards change from season to season, providing ample display time for all of the pieces over time.

If you like this . . . consider a visit to the Phoenix Art Museum on the northeast corner of Central Avenue and McDowell Road. The museum features more than 200,000 square feet of space, a sculpture garden, and works by Monet, Picasso, and Georgia O'Keeffe.

Late afternoon, end up at the Desert Botanical Garden (480-941-1225; www.dbg.org). Situated on 145 acres of land among the red-hued rocks at Papago Park, the garden is home to more than 50,000 arid-land plants (including almost 40 species of rare, threatened, or endangered plants from deserts across the globe). Located on the Phoenix-Tempe border near the Phoenix Zoo, it features thematic trails, desert wildflowers, numerous succulents, and tour guides to assist you in learning more about the plants and their natural environment. Hang around as the sun drops below the horizon and catch a glimpse of one of those sunsets Arizona is so famous for.

Dinner

You're in Arizona, so it's only natural to get a taste of our Southwestern cuisine. For an authentic Mexican food experience north of the border, you'll need to make Barrio Café (602-636-0240; www.barriocafe.com) a mandatory stop. At the Barrio—named Best Mexican

Quick tip: Visit the Heard Museum's Web site (www.heard.org) for information about live performances, like the Annual World Championship Hoop Dance Contest, and annual art shows and festivals. There are free public guided tours (45 minutes) daily.

The Heard Museum often hosts live events, like the Annual World Championship Hoop Dance Contest

Restaurant several years running by the *Arizona Republic*—Chef Silvana Salcido Esparza takes your palate south of any Mexican cuisine you might normally find in the Valley. While the menu might look familiar—tacos, enchiladas, tortas—these gourmet dishes are a cornucopia of ingredients that set your senses into overdrive. Located south of Thomas Road next to La Vacqueria de la Ropa and the discoteca, this storefront restaurant presents a medley of traditional Mexican decor (devotion candles dot the tables) and Mexican art by local artists; fans spin lazily above, and waiters make guacamole tableside while festive music blends with the laughter and voices in its crowded little rooms.

DAY 2

Breakfast/Early Lunch

La Grande Orange (602-840-7777; www.lagrandeorangegrocery.com) serves its meals Arizona style, with the doors thrown open, patio seating, and mountain views. This neighborhood favorite is set in Arcadia, an older Phoenix neighborhood. The café and grocery serves a plethora of dishes from oatmeal to crêpes; plus you can pick up gifts and keepsakes for home, including wine, locally made goods, and baked goodies, including Arizona favorites MJ Bread and Tammie Coe Cakes. Patio seating beneath a canopy of trees or beside the floor-to-ceiling windows embraces the desert setting of this local favorite as Camelback Mountain looms blocks away. The food is great, and the bustling atmosphere is enough to pump you up for another early-morning mountain hike!

If you like this . . . try Chelsea's Kitchen (602-957-2555; www.chelseas kitchenaz.com), at 40th Street north of Camelback, for Southwest-inspired brunch, lunch, or dinner.

> **Quick tip:** Park in front or in the back, where you enter through the kitchen.

Shopping

Since you're already over in the Biltmore area, take a trip among the fabulous upscale boutiques and shops you'll find at **Biltmore Fashion Park** (602-955-8400; www.shopbiltmore.com). More than 70 boutiques and restaurants line the courtyard garden, creating the perfect outdoor shopping experience. Well-known chains share space with specialty shops like This Little Piggy Wears Cotton, a delightful shop providing books, toys, and clothing for children through age 14, or Alessi, offering Italian home decor. The space is also home to major department stores Macy's and Saks Fifth Avenue, as well as national favorites Pottery Barn, Borders, Williams-Sonoma, and Ralph Lauren.

Lunch Before You Go

For a late lunch before you head to the airport, try **True Food Kitchen** (602-774-3488; www.foxrc.com/true_food _kitchen.html), only one of Fox Restaurant Concept's local successes. True is a joint effort between Arizona-based Fox and best-selling health guru Dr. Andrew Weil. The food is all natural, healthy fare from local and regional growers; the menu includes almost 30 vegetarian, vegan, or gluten-free items, from soups and salads to sandwiches, pizza, and pasta. Refreshments are au natural and include green teas, lemonades, and natural sodas; organic wines, spirits, and beer round out the menu. Located at Biltmore Fashion Park, True Food Kitchen also serves breakfast, brunch, and dinner.

Extend Your Stay

If you have more time, try these great places to see and things to do . . .

ARIZONA HERITAGE

Built in 1932 by William Wrigley Jr. (of the chewing gum conglomerate) for his wife, Ada, **Wrigley Mansion Club** (602-955-4079; www.wrigleymansion club.com), named La Colina Solana or "sunny hill," was one of the family's five homes and served as a winter cottage. While the 16,850-square-foot home with 24 rooms and 12 bathrooms embodies more splendor and opulence than you might associate with a "cottage," it was the smallest of the Wrigley homes and used two months out of the year at most. Wrigley Mansion remained in the family for 40 years and was once part of a portfolio of property owned by Tally Industries that included the Arizona Biltmore Resort and Golf Club, which rests below the 100-foot hill the mansion calls home. Tours are available Tuesday–Saturday; reserve your space for the one-hour tour by calling 602-955-4079.

The Wrigley Mansion Club, as it is now called, is technically a private club due to restrictions and regulations imposed upon it in 1982 when then-owner Western Savings made it a private club and corporate retreat. In 1992 the mansion once again changed hands and found itself owned by another well-known family—Geordie Hormel of the meatpacking Hormels. Hormel lowered club membership to just $10 per household, making it an affordable opportunity for just about anyone in the Valley, and 100 percent

Quick tip: The mansion is located northeast of 24th Street and Camelback at 2501 E. Telawa Trail and overlooks the Arizona Biltmore property. To get there, take 24th Street north of Camelback to Biltmore Circle, and take a right into the National Bank of Arizona parking lot. Past the bank is a white bridge that takes you to a switchback road that leads to the mansion. Park below and walk up or valet park at the top.

Quick tip: For more information, including a map of Phoenix's historic districts, visit online at www.ci.phoenix.az.us/HISTORIC /residents.html.

of the proceeds go to charity. The club is open for tours, and Geordie's Restaurant & Lounge is open for lunch and dinner on Friday and Saturday nights. The club serves an award-winning champagne brunch on Sunday. Mr. Hormel passed away in 2006 but has left a legacy here in the Valley.

In the late 1970s several older neighborhoods in the city of Phoenix decided to preserve their little pieces of history, when they lobbied for inclusion on the National Register of Historic Places. Since then a total of 35 neighborhoods in central Phoenix have been designated historic. Homeowners have taken great pride in restoring their homes to their previous splendor, and every year many of them open their homes to tours. Don't be discouraged if you miss the tours—a drive through these neighborhoods is an enjoyable experience for any lover of history or period homes. Some of these neighborhoods have been completely restored, while others are still in progress. The palm-lined avenues in the Encanto Park or the Willo District, west of Central Avenue, offer some of the most visually pleasing drives.

The Willo Historic District (www.willohistoricdistrict.com) is just west of Central Avenue between Thomas and McDowell roads, from First to Seventh avenues. The annual Willo Home Tour, held early February, offers a firsthand look at how residents have restored their homes to their original splendor. Built in the 1920s,

'30s, and '40s, these historic homes comprise bungalow-style as well as Tudor Revival, Greek Revival, American Colonial Revival, Spanish Colonial Revival, and Pueblo Revival. Homes built in the late 1930s are representative of French Provincial and Monterey styles; some homes are similar in architectural design to the modern-day ranch home. In the 1980s Willo residents lobbied to have their neighborhood preserved as a historic district. Between 12 and 14 neighborhood homes open their doors to the public for this event.

If you like this . . . try the Encanto Palmcroft Historic District (www.encantopalmcroft.org), located between Seventh and 15th avenues north of McDowell Road. They have a festival every other March (2011, 2013, etc.).

> **Quick tip:** Buy your tickets online and pick up at Will Call.

Located on the original town site of the city of Phoenix and listed on the National Register of Historic Places, Heritage Square (602-262-5071; www.phoenix.gov/PARKS/heritage.html) comprises several historic homes, restaurants, and shops, including the Victorian Rosson House museum built in 1895. The square shares space with the Arizona Science Center to create the Heritage & Science Park. Several events take place here throughout the year, including auto shows, holiday events, and cultural

> **Quick tip:** Call for hours; they vary depending upon the time of year.

events. Visit online for a calendar of events.

Named after the original owner, Dr. Roland Lee Rosson, the Rosson House (602-262-5070; recorded information 602-262-5029; www.rossonhousemuseum.org) was built in 1895, when he was mayor of Phoenix. However, Dr. Rosson resigned after only a year due to a disagreement with the city council; in 1897 he and his family sold their home and moved to Los Angeles. Today the Rosson House Museum has been restored to its original splendor and depicts life in the late 19th and early 20th centuries when Phoenix was still a territory. The home is almost 3,000 square feet, with 10 rooms and five fireplaces—large even by today's standards.

The Arizona Doll & Toy Museum (602-253-9337), in the Stevens House at Heritage Square, boasts a collection of dolls, dollhouses, and all things miniature. There's also a gift shop on-site.

ARTS & CULTURE

In 2006 the Phoenix Art Museum (602-257-1222 [24-hour information available] or 602-257-1880; www.phxart.org) completed a $50 million expansion. In addition to a new entrance off Central Avenue and a four-level gallery, the 2006 expansion included a new sculpture garden with 40,000 square feet of relaxing outdoor space in the heart of Phoenix and an expanded museum store. More than 17,000 works of modern, contemporary, and western American art and fashion design from across the globe make Phoenix Art Museum worth more than one trip. Opened in 1959, the original space has been expanded to incorporate 203,000 square feet. The museum's collection includes

Family-Friendly Phoenix

Teresa Bitler

Some of the Valley's most popular attractions cater to families.

A family-friendly exhibit at the Arizona Science Center

The **Musical Instrument Museum** (480-478-6000; www.themim.org) features interactive displays as well as an Experience Gallery, where children of all ages can touch, hear, and play musical instruments from around the globe.

At the world-renowned **Heard Museum** (602-251-0213; www.heard.org), kids can experience Native American culture through hands-on crafts and activities in three of the museum's 10 galleries.

Got a fire-truck fanatic in your family? Explore nearly an acre of fire history exhibits at the **Hall of Flame Museum of Firefighting** (602-275-3473; www.hallofflame.org), including the Fire Safety Learning Area and a 1951 engine. Don't forget the camera!

If you want to experience some of the Valley's history, check out the **Pueblo Grande Museum and Archaeological Park** (602-495-0901 or 877-706-4408; www.pueblogrande.org), where the family can learn about the prehistoric Hohokam people.

Or step back to the 1880s at **Rawhide Wild West Town** (480-502-5600; www.rawhide.com). Kids will enjoy the gunfights, desert train ride, Butterfield stagecoach, and burro rides. Best bet: sign up for a sundown cookout.

Who doesn't love animals? Voted one of the nation's top five zoos for kids, the **Phoenix Zoo** (602-273-1341; www.phoenixzoo.org) is home to approximately 1,300 animals, including two full-grown Komodo dragons.

In addition to the animals, the **World Wildlife Zoo & Aquarium** (623-935-9453; www.wildlifeworld.com) boasts a log flume ride, boat ride, carousel, and train ride.

Looking for a unique animal experience? Don't miss the new **Sea Life Aquarium** (480-478-7600; www.sealifeus.com /phoenix/phoenix-home), with its tunnel through a 165,000-gallon tank and 360-degree views.

Of course, the **Arizona Science Center** (602-716-2000; www.azscience.org) and the **Children's Museum of Phoenix** (602-253-0501; www.childrensmuseumofphoenix.org) are always family pleasers, with fun, interactive exhibits that engage the entire family.

The kid-friendly Children's Museum of Phoenix

Teresa Bitler is an Arizona mother of two and author of Great Escapes Arizona, *as well as two iPhone apps,* Family-Friendly Phoenix *and* Free & Budget Phoenix. *Her work has also appeared in* Sunset, Valley Guide, *the* Arizona Office of Tourism Newsletter, *and* Arizona Lifestyle *magazine.*

works from such greats as Monet, Picasso, and Georgia O'Keeffe. Changing exhibits have included Rembrandt and the Golden Age of Dutch Art, and Curves of Steel: Streamlined Automobile Design; these are often specially ticketed events.

The Musical Instrument Museum (480-478-6000; www.themim.org), the world's first ever museum dedicated to showcasing musical instruments from across the globe, opened in Phoenix in April 2010. The two-story museum is home to more than 10,000 instruments representing more than 200 countries and territories. Covering more than 190,000 square feet—75,000 of it dedicated to exhibits—the museum features a 299-seat acoustically sound auditorium designed to showcase musicians from around the world; the Experience Gallery, where children and adults alike are invited to play and listen to the sounds the instruments make; and 10 distinct galleries highlighting music from the 10 different regions of the world. Dedicated to the aural experience, the museum provides wireless earphones to use during your visit; the equipment is designed to pick up the audio playing when you step up to a particular display.

Phoenix Theatre (602-889-5284; www.phoenixtheatre.com), the oldest theater company in Arizona, was founded in 1920 as the Phoenix Players and is one of the oldest continuously operating arts groups in the United States. In 1923 the Phoenix Little Theatre, as it was called, found a permanent home at 100 E. McDowell in the stables of the Heard family homestead. In 1950, when the Heard family donated part of their land to Phoenix, the city agreed to keep Phoenix (Little) Theatre in place. In 1950 the current MainStage was completed, and the Phoenix Theatre grew into the professional company it is today. It's known for encouraging appreciation for theater and performs musicals, comedies, and drama, as well as productions just for kids through the 25-year-old Cookie Company Theatre for Young Audiences. Hollywood greats Nick Nolte and Steven Spielberg launched their careers from the Phoenix Theatre's MainStage, and the company continues to encourage new talent with their Artist-in-Residence Program.

OUTDOOR ADVENTURES

Ballooning

Sunny days and clear skies make for perfect ballooning weather, and the Phoenix metropolitan area offers tourists several options. The best time of year to go ballooning is between November and May, when weather is optimal. Morning trips leave just before sunrise; some companies also offer trips during the hotter months (June–October) two hours prior to sunset. Consider Rainbow Ryders (602-725-2477; www.rainbowryders.com), Over the Rainbow (602-225-5666; www.letsgoballooning.com), and Adventures Out West (800-755-0935;

Gardens & Nature Centers

An absolute must for Valley visitors, the Desert Botanical Garden (480-941-1225; www.dbg.org) is home to 50,000 arid-land plants (including 39 species that are endangered, rare, or threatened) from deserts all over the world. Situated among the red-hued rocks of Papago Park on the Phoenix-Tempe border, the garden boasts five thematic trails representing conservation, living in the desert, Sonoran Desert plants and people, and desert wildflowers. Several seasonal events, including the annual butterfly and wildflower exhibits, reveal just how colorful the desert can be in spring. The site also features a garden shop (480-481-8113) and library (480-481-8133). Enjoy live jazz music fall and spring at the Patio Café (480-941-1225). Guided tours are available daily October–May; bird walks occur weekly year-round; and to enjoy the garden in summer, partake in a sunrise or flashlight tour.

The Nina Mason Pulliam Rio Salado Audubon Center (602-468-6470; http://az.audubon.org) officially opened its doors in the fall of 2009. Designed to support one of Audubon's key missions—connecting urban children with nature—the center sits on the 600-acre parcel of land designated as the City of Phoenix Rio Salado Habitat Restoration Area. Located on the south side of the Salt River on the east side of Central, the center is uniquely positioned to provide educational programs, field trips, and community resources to area residents, both children and adults. The center's unique architecture is not only visually stunning, it was also specifically designed to minimally impact the environment.

Hiking

To hike in these parts, you don't need to go far, no matter what part of the Valley you're in. All of the biking paths mentioned earlier double as hiking trails, including Papago Park and Phoenix South Mountain Preserve.

Papago Park (www.phoenix.gov /PARKS/hikpagud.html) is a popular site located on the border of Phoenix and Tempe. The park is home to the Phoenix Zoo and Desert Botanical Garden. Its central location and easy paths with little or no elevation change make it a popular hiking and biking choice. To hike around Papago Buttes, park on W. Park Drive, and to explore the famous Hole in the Rock—a natural opening in the red-rock

There are many places to hike in and around the Phoenix area

butte—park just past the zoo at the information center. The park's trails range from 0.1 mile (Hole-in-the-Rock Trail) to 4 miles (West Park Loop Trail).

Some of the best hiking trails can be found at the South Mountain Park and Preserve (www.phoenix.gov /PARKS/hiksogud.html). With incredible views and easy accessibility, you would think that the preserve would be overrun with hiking, biking, and horseback-riding enthusiasts; however, 58 trails on 16,000 acres leaves plenty of room to roam. While paths close to the entrances tend to be busy, the crowds thin out as you head farther from the trailheads. Mormon Trail (24th Street and Valley View Avenue south of Baseline Road) is 1.1 miles at an elevation of about 1,000 feet. Beverly Canyon Trail (8800 S. 46th Street south of Baseline Road) is a 1.5-mile-long, moderate hike with some steep sections. Javelina Canyon Trail (Beverly Canyon parking lot at 46th Street) is an easy to moderate hike at 1.7 miles

long. Pima Canyon is located at 9904 S. 48th Street and Guadalupe Road (Guadalupe cannot be accessed off I-10; instead take the Elliot Road exit, take Elliot to 48th Street, and head north to the park road, which is set somewhat off the street on the west side). Hikers at Pima Canyon can choose several trails, including the aforementioned Beverly Canyon Trail, the 14.3-mile National Trail, and the 9-mile Desert Classic Trail. Both of the latter trails are moderate to difficult.

From Desert Foothills Parkway just north of Chandler Boulevard (head west of 48th Street on Chandler until you reach Desert Foothills Parkway, then go north to Sixth Street), access Telegraph Pass Trailhead. The first 0.5 mile of the trail is paved. While there are some steep sections toward the top, the 1.5-mile trail is easy to moderate. The Holbert Trailhead, accessible from Central, is located at the Activity Complex (the first left turn immediately after entering the park off Central).

Biltmore Fashion Park (602-955-8400; www.shopbiltmore.com) features more than 60 boutiques and restaurants along its courtyard-style sidewalks, offering a collection of upscale options like Gucci, Tommy Bahama, Ann Taylor, and Escada; department stores Macy's and Saks Fifth Avenue; as well as Borders Books and Music. Find gourmet cookware at Williams-Sonoma, out-of-the-ordinary fixtures at Restoration Hardware, designer tea and complementary accessories at Teavana, lotions and candles at L'Occitane en Provence, hand-blown glassware at BeDazzled Gallery, and high-quality clothing, books, and toys for newborns to 14-year-olds at This Little Piggy Wears Cotton.

But Biltmore Fashion Park offers more than a unique shopping experience—you can meet for coffee at Paradise Bakery, lunch at the Cheesecake Factory (anticipate a wait) or California Pizza Kitchen, dine on oysters and sushi at Steamer's Genuine Seafood, or thoroughly pamper yourself at Elizabeth Arden Red Door Spa.

Phoenix's Chinatown—the COFCO Chinese Cultural Center (602-275-8578; www.phxchinatown .com)—offers a unique combination of Asian restaurants and shops. The Super L Ranch Market, a grocery store, sells traditional Asian foods, items imported from Asia, fresh produce, and baked goods. They boast the freshest seafood in Phoenix. Asian restaurants at the center include the Golden Buddha (Cantonese and Mandarin), Lao Ching Hing (Shanghai style), and Szechwan Palace (spicy Szechuan). Together, shops like Asian Video/Audio (five thousand CDs, DVDs, VCDs, and cassettes in Chinese make it one of the

Outdoor shopping at Desert Ridge Marketplace, north Phoenix

Arizona Center is an urban oasis in downtown Phoenix

largest stores of its kind in the nation); Oriental Factory Direct, which offers imported goods from Hong Kong, Thailand, and other Asian ports at bargain prices; the Chinese Herbal Shop; and Golden Gifts (bonsai trees, bamboo, and vases) create a unique shopping experience. Stroll through the energy-balanced landscape of the Gardens, designed by famous garden architect Madame Ye.

Energetic, fast paced, and *huge* are the three terms that best describe Desert Ridge Marketplace (480-513-7586; www.shopdesertridge.com). This 1.3-million-square-foot entertainment complex, the ultimate master-planned community, has several gated commu-

Did you know? Ye incorporated both feng shui and yin–yang principles in her designs to create a harmonious atmosphere for guests as they wander among the carefully sculpted grounds.

nities, golf courses, five separate shopping districts, and plenty of restaurants. A stay at the Marriott here gives the term *vacation package* a whole new meaning. Desert Ridge features a beautifully landscaped open-air marketplace with an 18-screen cinema, rock-climbing wall, bowling alley, dozens of nationally recognized shops, and a couple of local favorites.

The two-story open-air Arizona Center (602-271-4000; www.arizona center.com), located in downtown Phoenix between Van Buren and Fillmore streets and Third and Fifth streets, features shops; restaurants like Sam's Café, Mi Amigos, and Hooters; and a 24-theater AMC Cineplex in the heart of downtown Phoenix. The urban setting, meandering paths, towering palm trees, and a fantastic waterfall and fountain all make for a great outdoor shopping and dining experience.

Also downtown is CityScape (www.cityscapephoenix.com), a recently built, mixed-use urban development project featuring shopping, dining, and entertainment in the center of downtown—at the corner of Washington and Central. Laugh it up at Stand Up Live, the Valley's newest comedy club; go bowling at Lucky Strike Lanes; or hit any one of the restaurants, bars, or eateries.

SPORTS SCENE

Golf

The Phoenix area's three-hundred-plus days a year of sun and incredible scenery make it a top choice for vacationers of all backgrounds and activity levels. And many visitors (serious enthusiasts and dabblers alike) agree that a game of golf and a bit of pampering are essential parts of any vacation in the Valley—especially when the neighbors back home are shivering under a foot of snow!

From city facilities to championship courses designed by some of golf's greatest players, any of the Valley's two hundred courses—with their blue skies and mountain backdrops—are worthy of a game. Whether golf is an obsession or an occasional indulgence, you will find a range of course styles, prices, and locations that challenge your skills and provide ample enjoyment until you can return for another round.

The San Marcos Golf Resort in Chandler opened in 1913, and with it Arizona's oldest grass golf course was born. This 18-hole golf course has challenged presidents, dignitaries, and celebrities; it now operates as the Crowne Plaza San Marcos Golf Resort. The rich golf tradition started by the San Marcos echoes in many of the Valley's golf courses, including the Wigwam Golf Resort and Spa in Litchfield; the Arizona Biltmore Golf Club, adjacent to Arizona Biltmore Resort; the Phoenix Country Club—original home

Did you know? The Adobe Course at the Arizona Biltmore Golf Club was designed by William Bell back in 1929, when the resort was first built.

of the Phoenix Open (now the Waste Management Open); and The Players' Club (TPC) Scottsdale, the current home of the Waste Management Open.

The Arizona Biltmore Golf Club (602-955-9655; www.azbiltmoregc .com) is one of the area's more well-known courses. Set in the heart of the Biltmore District adjacent to the Arizona Biltmore, this country club is a local favorite featuring incredible views and two championship courses.

In north Phoenix, Dove Valley Ranch Golf Club (480-473-1444; www.dovevalleyranch.com) is an 18-hole desert course designed by Trent Jones Jr. and built in 1998.

In south Phoenix is one of Arizona's best ranked courses: the Raven Golf Club at South Mountain (602-243-3636; www.theravensouthmoun tain.com), a pine-tree-lined golf course reminiscent of a midwestern-style course.

Spectator Sports

Greater Phoenix is one of the few cities with four major-league sports teams: the Phoenix Coyotes (NHL), Arizona Cardinals (NFL), Phoenix Suns (NBA), and Arizona Diamondbacks (MLB). In addition, the city hosts other major teams, including the Phoenix Mercury (WNBA), as well as several major sporting events, including the Waste Management Open, two NASCAR events, spring training, and Arizona State University Division I sports. In 2008 the Valley hosted Super Bowl XLII at University of Phoenix Stadium in Glendale. The Valley also offers thoroughbred racing, arena football, and the Indy Racing League.

The Arizona Cardinals play September–December. After sharing ASU's Sun Devil Stadium for years, the Cardinals have finally moved into University of Phoenix Stadium (1 Cardinals Drive, Glendale). For game schedules and ticket information, call 602-379-0102 or visit www.azcardinals.com. The Phoenix Coyotes play at Glendale Arena. For game dates and ticket information, call 623-850-PUCK or visit www.phoenixcoyotes.com. The NBA Phoenix Suns (602-379-SUNS; www .phoenixsuns.com) play October–April, and the WNBA Phoenix Mercury (602-379-7878; www.phoenixmercury .com) play May–August at US Airways Center in downtown Phoenix. The Arizona Diamondbacks (602-514-8400; www.azdiamondbacks.com) play April–October at Chase Field in downtown Phoenix. Indy Racing League in March and NASCAR events in April and November take place at Phoenix International Raceway (602-252-2227; www.phoenixintlraceway.com). ASU Athletics (480-965-2381; www.asu.edu) Pac-10 sports take place between August and May. The Insight Bowl (480-350-0911; www.insightbowl.com), an NCAA football game, occurs in December, and the Fiesta Bowl (480-350-0911; www.tostitosfiestabowl.com), now at University of Phoenix Stadium in Glendale, typically falls in late December or early January. See "Glendale and the West Valley" for

more information about University of Phoenix Stadium.

Spring training in Arizona calls out more than a million baseball fans each year. It is not uncommon for local residents to skip out of work on a Friday afternoon to catch a game—or for avid sports fans to follow their teams to Arizona for the duration of spring training. The Cactus League hosts 17 teams at 12 stadiums in the Valley. Both the Milwaukee Brewers (623-245-5500; http://milwaukee.brewers.mlb.com) and the Oakland A's (602-392-0217; www.oaklandathletics.com) play in Phoenix. The Brewers play on the west side of Phoenix at Maryvale Baseball Park at 51st Avenue, and the Oakland A's play close to the Tempe-Phoenix border at Phoenix Municipal Stadium.

For more information about spring training in Arizona, visit www.cactus-league.com, or see each team's individual site. Ticket prices start at $5 and are available online from each team's site, on-site, or by phone.

To find out more about where your favorite team plays, visit the following chapters: Arizona Diamondbacks, Colorado Rockies, and San Francisco Giants ("Scottsdale"); Anaheim Angels and Chicago Cubs ("Tempe and the East Valley"); and Arizona Cardinals, Chicago White Sox, Cincinnati Reds, Cleveland Indians, Kansas City Royals, Los Angeles Dodgers, Phoenix Coyotes, San Diego Padres, Seattle Mariners, and Texas Rangers ("Glendale and the West Valley").

2

Scottsdale
FOUNTAIN HILLS, PARADISE VALLEY, CAVE CREEK, CAREFREE

Host to more than 125 art galleries and 60 public artworks, Scottsdale is the sophisticated sister to the rest of the Valley. The city features hundreds of upscale restaurants, boutiques, and shops, and boasts a number of the Valley's top resorts, golf courses, and spas. Nestled between both Camelback and Mummy mountains and set against the magnificent McDowell Mountains, it is home to several of the Valley's five-diamond resorts. Take a seat at one of its many pools, and you will find yourself in an oasis of palm trees, blue skies, and mountain backdrops. Enjoy a plethora of dining options; there are more than six hundred—from the eclectic indie restaurant Cowboy Ciao to the solid steakhouse experience at Mastro's City Hall Steakhouse (480-941-4700; www.mastrosrestaurants.com). Rub shoulders with sports stars, movie stars, famous authors, and celebrities of all kinds; many of the Valley's VIPs have made this beautiful city home. Experience the greatest show on grass—the Waste Management Open at TPC in North Scottsdale—or the famous Barrett Jackson Auto Show. Shop at any number of unique outdoor malls, including Shops at Gainey Ranch, el Pedregal, or the Waterfront, or spend hours wandering the sidewalks of Old Town Scottsdale's shopping and arts districts, visiting the numerous art galleries, cafés, restaurants, shops, and boutiques selling

Did you know? Fountain Hills' famous man-made fountain was developed as a landmark for this community in the early 1970s and uses recycled and reclaimed water from the 28-acre lake surrounding it. It's located in Fountain Park at the heart of the community and shoots 560 feet into the desert air. The uniquely designed nozzle weighs 2,000 pounds and can conduct 375 pounds of water per square inch—at a rate of 7,000 gallons a minute—to heights unmatched throughout the world. At present the fountain operates 15 times a day, as weather and wind velocity permit. For 10 minutes every hour on the hour 10 AM–9 PM daily, this is an amazing sight to behold.

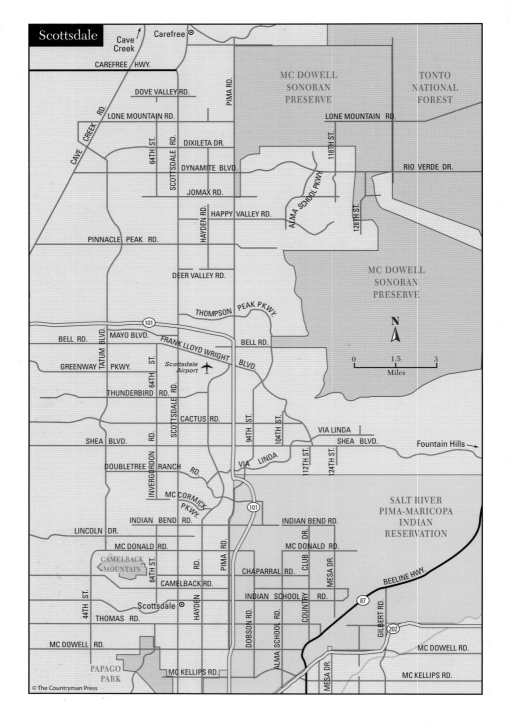

Scottsdale

© The Countryman Press

everything from high-priced original art to Native American handiwork to locally designed apparel and accessories.

Scottsdale also touches on Fountain Hills—a small community to the east of North Scottsdale and home to the famous fountain—located on the eastern slope of the McDowell Mountains; Cave Creek and Carefree, sister cities north of Phoenix and Scottsdale; and Paradise Valley, nestled along the Phoenix-Scottsdale border.

The Scottsdale and Paradise Valley area is home to a number of resort properties that draw visitors from around the world. No two are alike.

Pick Your Spot

Best places to stay in Scottsdale, and what you'll find nearby . . .

PARADISE VALLEY

Nestled in Paradise Valley, an island of luxury living in the middle of north Phoenix, is the InterContinental Montelucia Resort & Spa (602-956-9400; www.montelucia.com). Situated against the majestic backdrop of Camelback Mountain, this resort, reminiscent of a Spanish village, offers a true luxury resort experience with a 30,000-square-foot spa, several upscale dining options, on-site concierge staff, and easy access to the upscale Biltmore shopping and dining district.

Also in Paradise Valley, the Sanctuary on Camelback Mountain resort and spa (800-245-2051; www.sanctuaryoncamelback.com) has been voted the number one resort in the United States by *Condé Nast Traveler* readers. Located on Camelback Mountain, Sanctuary lives up to its name and affords a relaxing escape to those who stay in one of its 98 casitas. The resort features amazing views of the city and mountain landscape just north of the upscale Biltmore District. Sanctuary Spa offers both indoor and outdoor treatment rooms, a meditation garden, and a therapeutic pool. Dine on-site at well-known elements restaurant, or relax at the jade bar.

The infinity pool at Sanctuary on Camelback Mountain   Photo courtesy of Sanctuary on Camelback Mountain

Millennium Resort Scottsdale McCormick Ranch (480-948-5050 or 800-243-1332; www.milleniumhotels.com/milleniumscottsdale/index.html) features 125 rooms and 51 villas. Combined with magnificent views, a lakefront location, and award-winning golf, it's a top choice for Scottsdale visitors. Golf lovers can work with golf sales manager Michael Luna, the resort's on-site "golf concierge," to plan custom golf tours of some of the area's most exclusive courses.

If you like this . . . read the Custom Golf Tours *sidebar later in this chapter.*

A desert oasis in North Scottsdale, close to the Loop 101 and Kierland Commons, the Fairmont Scottsdale Princess (480-585-4848 or 800-344-4758; www.fairmont.com/scottsdale) provides a wonderful escape from the rest of the world. Relax beside one of several pools with beverage service. It's located adjacent to TPC of Scottsdale, with an on-site spa that brings the full Scottsdale experience to you.

In the shadows of Pinnacle Peak, high above North Scottsdale, lies Four Seasons Resort Scottsdale at Troon North (480-515-5700 or 888-207-9696; www.fourseasons.com/scottsdale), with enchanting city views, a restaurant and bar, poolside service, on-site tennis, horseback riding, hiking, golf, and spa. Guest suites and casitas are available. This is a Four Seasons experience set in the rugged Sonoran Desert.

Westin Kierland Resort & Spa (480-624-1000 or 800-WESTIN-1; www.kierlandresort.com) offers an on-site spa and salon, three nine-hole golf courses, and a complimentary fitness center, as well as a teen club, kids' club, and 8,000-square-foot pool, complete with a zero-entry sandy beach, a 110-foot water slide, and a flowing river ride. To top it off, the Westin Kierland is adjacent to the 38-acre Kierland Commons shopping and dining extravaganza. The 732-room resort

Golf at Westin Kierland

Photo courtesy of Westin Kierland Resort & Spa

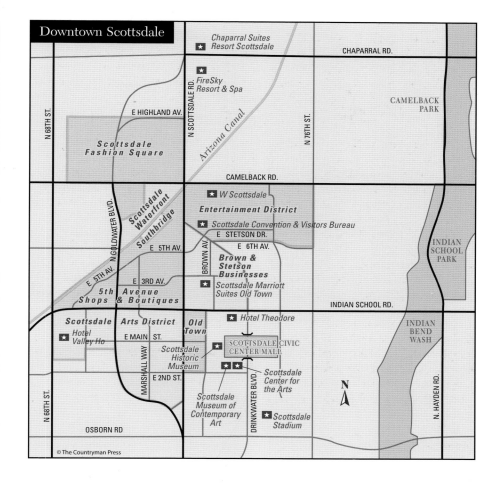

Downtown Scottsdale

© The Countryman Press

features 55 suites and 32 casita units, along with nine dining experiences, including Deseo, which serves Latin-influenced cuisine under the direction of award-winning chef Douglas Rodriguez.

DOWNTOWN SCOTTSDALE

In downtown Scottsdale, there are a number of brand name accommodations, as well as several urban hotels, that offer first-class service to accompany their terrific location in the heart of Scottsdale's thriving arts, dining, and entertainment districts.

Hotel Valley Ho (480-248-2000 or 866-882-4484; www.hotelvalleyho.com), originally built in 1956, has been renovated into an urban oasis with 194 rooms and a 1950s Rat Pack–era style that rarely breaks character (it's retro, hip, and techno-savvy). Amenities include complimentary wireless Internet access; morning espresso, tea, and coffee; on-site fitness room; and a courtyard pool inspired by a martini.

If you like this . . . consider requesting an architectural tour of the property.

Built in 1956, Hotel Valley Ho has retained its unflappable Rat Pack image

Did you know? VH (Vitality +
Health) Spa offers various body
treatments, manicures, pedicures,
facials, and massages—perhaps a
hot shell massage. Travelers can
also work out in the open-air fitness studio overlooking the pool;
yoga and Pilates classes are available throughout the week.

Pool at W Scottsdale at night

The new W Scottsdale (480-970-
2100; www.starwoodhotels.com/whotels
/scottsdale) embodies the glitz and
glamour of Scottsdale. The boutique
hotel features 224 rooms and a deck-
top pool—with portholes to the lobby
below—overlooking downtown Scottsdale. Indulge in the on-site spa or dine
on fresh sushi at Sushi Roku.

The latest addition to Scottsdale's urban core is Hotel Theodore (480-308-
1100; www.hoteltheodore.com). Most recently the Mondrian, this hotel is located
in the heart of Scottsdale's Old Town district and opens onto the Scottsdale Civic
Plaza via its onsite Italian restaurant Cielo. It's a short walk from any number of
great shops, restaurants, galleries, bars, and clubs.

A mere 3 blocks north of downtown Scottsdale and Scottsdale Fashion Square is Kimpton's FireSky Resort & Spa (480-945-7666; www.fireskyresort.com), a warm, welcoming, pet-friendly oasis in the middle of Scottsdale. The resort's homage to the four elements—earth, fire, water, and air—are reflected in the indoor and outdoor fireplaces, lagoon-style pools, lush landscaping, and soaring ceilings. Dine on the delicious Italian-coastal cuisine on-site at Taggia or partake in various relaxing treatments at Jurlique Spa. A little farther north is the four-diamond, 22-acre Doubletree Paradise Valley Resort/Scottsdale (480-947-5400; www.paradise valley.doubletree.com).

CAREFREE

The 1,300-acre Boulders Resort and Golden Door Spa (480-488-9009 or 800-553-1717; www.theboulders.com) has received numerous accolades, earning it a top spot for Valley visitors from the world over. An award-winning spa, two championship golf courses designed by Jay Moorish, eight tennis courts, five dining experiences, and one bar—not to mention incredible views of the Sonoran Desert—make it a true destination resort. To top it off, they offer excellent golf, spa, and summer packages. The resort features 160 casitas and one-, two-, and three-bedroom villas.

Located in the foothills of the Continental Mountains, just north of Scottsdale, Carefree Resort & Villas (888-692-4343; www.carefree-resort.com) embodies

FireSky Resort & Spa's oasis in the desert

Taggia at FireSky Resort in Scottsdale

Photo courtesy of Kimpton's FireSky Resort & Spa

Western-style charm and hospitality. Twenty-six acres of Sonoran Desert, golf at nearby Legend Trails, and the new Spa at Carefree Resort & Villas all make for a relaxing experience in a beautiful setting.

FOUNTAIN HILLS

A small luxury resort, CopperWynd Resort and Club (480-333-1848 or 877-707-7760; www.copperwynd.com) features breathtaking views from its 32 mountainside guest rooms; in-room amenities include gas-burning fireplace, wireless Internet access, and private balcony. There are also 10 villas.

A Santa Fe–style property set in the Sonoran Desert, the Inn at Eagle Mountain (480-816-3000 or 800-992-8083; www.innateaglemountain.com) is located above the 18th green of the prestigious Golf Club at Eagle Mountain and features 42 minisuites with fireplace, private deck, and whirlpool tub for two. The resort offers golf packages.

NATIVE AMERICAN INDIAN COMMUNITIES

Casino lovers have a couple of options. The brand new, 15-story Talking Stick Resort (480-850-7777; www.talkingstickresort.com) at Casino Arizona is owned by the Salt River Pima-Maricopa Indian Community and adjacent to the Talking Stick Golf Club. Alternatively, the Radisson Fort McDowell Resort & Casino (480-789-5300 or 800-715-0328; www.radissonfortmcdowellresort.com), owned by the Fort McDowell Yavapai Nation, is tucked behind the McDowell Mountains near Fountain Hills. It features 248 guest rooms and suites, and offers high-speed Internet access, a pool, and a fitness facility. The on-site Anhala Restaurant and Lounge features dishes made with locally grown citrus, pecans, herbs, and mesquite from the Fort McDowell Yavapai Farm.

Fast fact: The Talking Stick Resort is located across the Loop 101 from the Arizona Diamondbacks's and Colorado Rockies's new spring training facility.

Local Flavors

Taste of the town . . . local restaurants, cafés, bars, bistros, etc.

RESTAURANTS

Paradise Valley

Just as cowboy artist Alonzo (Lon) Megargee lassoed the beauty of the Southwest and spread it out on canvas for others to enjoy, Executive Chef Jeremy Pacheco has successfully captured the tastes of the West and artistically arranges their flavors with flair for his guests' enjoyment at LON's at the Hermosa (602-955-7878; www.lons .com). The restaurant has garnered local and national acclaim for its culinary artistry. Enjoy dishes like prickly pear glazed California lamb chops or fennel dusted organic salmon on the beautiful patio beneath the mesquite trees in the radiating warmth of the outdoor fireplace. The restaurant, located in the shadows of Camelback Mountain as part of the Hermosa Inn compound, hosts an artist-in-residence series in keeping with the artistic image of Lon Megargee. Past guests have included author Aaron Elkins, musician Tito Puente Jr., and artists David L. Bradley and Victor Ostrovsky. Guests can purchase tickets ($125 per person, plus tax and gratuity) to attend. For reservations, call 602-955-7878.

North Scottsdale

A Scottsdale landmark, HandlebarJ Restaurant & Saloon (480-948-0110; www.handlebarj.com) has been providing locals and tourists alike with a wild, Western time since 1966. Steaks, barbecue ribs, homemade biscuits, and corn-on-the cob combined with live country music and country dance les-

sons make it an authentic "out West" experience. Wednesday–Sunday the Herndon Brothers Band plays starting at 8:30 PM; live music Monday and Tuesday; free country dance lessons Wednesday, Thursday, and Sunday starting at 7 PM.

Chow down on burgers and steaks cowboy style at Reata Pass Steakhouse/Greasewood Flat (480-585-7277; www.reatapass.com), a 120-year-old bunkhouse-turned-restaurant. Located at Reata Pass—a stagecoach stop between Fort McDowell and Phoenix back when Phoenix was a long

LON's at the Hermosa

and dusty 30-mile ride away—this is a steakhouse and saloon (Greasewood Flat) where the tables are picnic and the steaks are grilled to perfection.

South Scottsdale

When the menu comes with a heat chart, you know they're serious about spicy. You'll find New Mexican cuisine with lots of chiles—both green and red—in the out-of-the-way Carlsbad Tavern & Restaurant (480-970-8164; www.carlsbadtavern.com), located off Hayden Road. Sit inside or outside on the patio, where you'll often hear live acoustic music. They have a late-night menu, so stop by anytime before 2 AM. House specialties include Carlsbad Pasta, chipotle barbecue baby back ribs, and pecanwood-grilled fish; steaks and burgers and enchiladas, too. Everything has pizzazz, so just ask them to dial up or down according to your tastes. It's located in a mostly residential neighborhood, so you'll miss it if you're not looking for it on the east side of the road, south of Osborn between Thomas and Indian School roads.

The Salt Cellar (480-947-1963; www.saltcellarrestaurant.com) is literally nothing to look at. When you drive up, you'll wonder how the tiny shack could serve perhaps the best seafood in town. But looks can be deceiving. What you see is simply the entrance; the rest of the place is three flights underground. While the dress is casual, the food is anything but. Delicious seafood is flown in fresh daily from places like Georges Bank, Chesapeake Bay, and the Gulf of Mexico: the freshest trout, lobster, ahi, sea bass, scallops, king crab—and the list goes on. They also serve sumptuous steaks, including filet mignon and beef Wellington. White tablecloths, fantastic servers, and elegant dishes share space in this enchanting little restaurant. Reservations are highly recommended. Should you arrive early, enjoy a drink at the full bar; on weekends space is tight.

Downtown Scottsdale

Think out of the box, and you have Cowboy Ciao (480-WINE-111; www.cowboyciao.com)—an eclectic mix of personality, panache, and amazing food in an environment as bold as its flavors. One visit will having you begging for more—more food, more fun, and more of whatever it is they're putting in the wine. Sister hot spot Kazimierz World Wine Bar is located close by, and any combination will provide a fun, relaxing, and satiating experience of excellent food paired with great spirits and, well . . . the company you share is up to you.

A family owned neighborhood favorite, Frank and Lupe's (480-990-9844; www.frankandlupes.com) is the offspring of Frank and Lupe's in Socorro, New Mexico. Owned and operated by their sons Eddie and Ted Bernal, it's been featured in *Bon Appétit* and *Gourmet* magazines. The laid-back atmosphere and colorful decor invite an appetizing experience of delicious New Mexican fare and wonderful margaritas. The chips and guacamole make an excellent appetizer; however, they have plenty of choices, including tamales, burritos, chiles rellenos, and enchiladas, all spiced with varying degrees of heat, for those looking for a full meal.

At Arcadia Farms (480-941-5665; www.arcadiafarmscafe.com), owner Carolyn Ellis has created a delightful dining experience in this charming little downtown tea-room-style café; lunch is meant to be savored. The salads are wonderful medleys of fruits, greens, nuts, cheeses, and veggies drizzled with vinaigrette dressings; the

Old Town versus Downtown

What makes Old Town Scottsdale such a unique destination—for tourists, travelers and residents alike—is that you can find a little bit (and sometimes a lot) of everything. From Native American art to contemporary art, country music to techno, wine bars to cowboy bars, upscale restaurants to inexpensive cafés, and Barneys to boutique shops you won't find anywhere else in the world. And it's all concentrated in an area that's perhaps 2 to 3 square miles in the heart of Scottsdale.

"Old Town" Scottsdale is made up of five districts that meld and flow into one another, each with a distinct personality: The Fifth Avenue Shopping District, world-renowned Marshall Way Contemporary Arts District, Main Street Arts & Antiques District, Old Town (the city's origins), and the Brown & Stetson Business District. There's also the Waterfront and Fashion Square Mall on Camelback. These areas are easily navigated on foot (or by trolley, which is free) and are peppered with specialty shops, bars, restaurants, and art galleries.

Ride the free trolley through downtown Scottsdale

But, while Old Town Scottsdale is the name often used to describe all five districts (plus the recently developed Waterfront), technically, it's only one section and is comprised of the 40 acres originally subdivided by Rhode Island transplant Albert G. Utley in 1894. He named the city Scottsdale after U.S. Army chaplain Winfield Scott, who played a monumental role in encouraging the first settlers to make this area their new home.

delicious sandwiches are built for two; and house specialties include wild mushroom, spinach, and goat cheese tart, and fresh lump crabcakes. If you have the chance try one of her other successes—each featuring a unique menu and a different kind of experience—check out Arcadia Farms locations at the Phoenix Art Museum and Center Bistro at the Scottsdale Center for the Performing Arts. Reservations are suggested at the downtown Scottsdale location, which is located 1 block south of Indian School Road, between Goldwater Boulevard and Scottsdale Road.

Malee's on Main (480-947-6042; www.maleesonmain.com) is nestled among the art galleries and shops of the Main Street Arts & Antiques District in a 1921 building that has been a teahouse, a French restaurant, and an Italian eatery. Today it's a Thai bistro serving an array of exotic dishes and sushi. Keep in mind that Thai spicy is not the same as salsa spicy, so when you tell them, "No problem, I can handle it," you may want to think twice. Their "mild" spicy is *hot;* anything more, and you may need to use your napkin to mop your brow. Delicious Thai cuisine with a kick.

CAFÉS & EATERIES

North Scottsdale

Blu Burger Grille (480-948-3443 [N. Scottsdale Road] and 480-585-0454 [E. Jomax Road]; www.bluburger .com) puts a whole new kind of spin on the traditional fast-food burger experience—in fact, they've elevated it past fast food altogether. These are gourmet burgers. Choose the meat, the way it's cooked, and all the toppings. With what a fast-food meal costs these days, the prices aren't bad, and you might be able to skip your next meal!

Downtown Scottsdale

The Breakfast Club (480-222-2582; www.thebreakfastclub.us) features a great little barista bar (they make the best café mochas in town) and a Southwest-infused breakfast and lunch menu.

Daily Dose (480-994-3673; www.dailydosegrill.com), owned by local restaurant veterans Matt and JennLyn Long, doubles as a neighborhood restaurant and bar with food that demands your taste buds pay attention—try the Hangover Sandwich or the peach crème brûlée pancakes, or one of their omelets or . . . you get the picture. The dishes are decadent and delicious, whether you're there for breakfast, lunch, or dinner. Breakfast is served 7–4 daily and followed by a half-price happy hour, buckets of beer, and Häagen-Dazs milk shakes.

Orange Table Café (480-424-6819; 7373 Scottsdale Mall, Suite 6) has been featured in the *New York Times* and *USA Today,* as well as local media outlets like *Sonoran Living* and *Desert Living,* and serves breakfast and lunch. Their wacky menu includes four different types of corned beef hash and eight different versions of pancakes (who knew you could get jalapeños in pancakes?). Plus they have homemade granola, omelets, sandwiches, and—

well, you'll just have to check it out for yourself.

Sugar Bowl Ice Cream Parlor & Restaurant (480-946-0051; 4005 N. Scottsdale Road) has been keeping the heat at bay for Valley residents since 1958 with its delicious assortment of cold treats; they also serve old-fashioned American fare.

WINE BARS

Scottsdale is a haven for wine lovers.

North Scottsdale

Check out Uncorked! The Unpretentious Wine Bar (480-629-9230; www.uncorkedwinebar.com) in North Scottsdale, where it's all about you and your palate. Choose from 50 wines by the glass and bottle, and discover the right wine for your tastes. No worries for beer lovers; this wine bar also serves beer (draft and bottled), as well as a light menu of sandwiches, cheese plates, and salads.

Downtown Scottsdale

The award-winning Su Vino Winery (480-994-VINO; www.suvinowinery az.com), originally founded in Grapevine, Texas, is located in the arts district of Old Town Scottsdale, not far from Malee's (look for the golden dome, and you'll see the sign pointing the way). They serve their own wines (many by the glass or bottle) and offer inexpensive tastings—$10 for five wines—on a variety of choices you won't find anywhere else. They also offer a fantastic little menu with appetizers and desserts meant to complement their unique and flavorful blends. The owners and their staff are wonderfully helpful, so don't be shy; they're happy to answer your questions, recommend a wine, or even develop a custom wine perfect for your palate.

Kazimierz World Wine Bar (480-946-3004; www.kazbar.net; 7137 E. Stetson Dr.) has a wine list the size of a novel, as well as great appetizers and cheese plates. It's so hip, you can't find it unless someone shows you the secret entrance. To get there, take Scottsdale Road to Stetson Drive (just south of Camelback Road); go west on Stetson and park along the street (or valet). On Stetson across the street from the Estate House and down from Cowboy Ciao is an outdoor corridor with a sign that says STETSON PLAZA above it. Head down the corridor and turn left. You'll see a wooden door with a sign reading the TRUTH IS INSIDE. You've made it.

Also check out the fairly new 5th and Wine (480-699-8001; www.5th andwine.com), a restaurant and wine lounge.

Private seating at Orange Sky Lounge at Talking Stick Resort

48 Hours

If you don't have much time to spend here, or if you've only allocated a couple of days of your vacation to the Scottsdale area, this short-trip itinerary, which centers around Frank Lloyd Wright's well-known feat of architecture, Taliesin West, will give you an idea of what to do while you're here. While two days is not enough time to do everything here, it's plenty of time to catch some of the best of what the area offers.

GETTING THERE

Frank Lloyd Wright's Taliesin West (480-860-2700; www.franklloydwright .org) is located in north Scottsdale off Cactus Road and the aptly named Frank Lloyd Wright Boulevard. To get there, take the Loop 101 to Cactus Road. Head east on Cactus until it turns into Taliesin Drive just east of Frank Lloyd Wright Boulevard. Follow the road until you reach parking.

Consider a nighttime tour of the property, located on the north side of town. The two-hour Night Lights on the Desert tour, which begin sometime between 6 and 7:30 PM, depending upon the time of year (this tour does not run in November or December), includes light refreshments to hold you over for a late dinner. At night the property lights up, transforming the daytime architecture into a stunning display with a twinklelit view of the Valley.

Complement your architectural tour with a late dinner at one of the Valley's newest and highest restaurants—Orange Sky Lounge at the Talking Stick Resort on Salt River Pima-Maricopa Indian Community land (see *Pick Your Spot*). Located on

Quick tip: If you're up for a little gambling, head back downstairs to the resort's on-site casino.

the 15th floor of the resort at Indian Bend and the Loop 101, Orange Sky Lounge features upscale dining and first-class seating with private banquettes and panoramic views of the city and Sonoran Desert below.

DAY 1

Golf or Spa

If you're staying in Scottsdale, chances are you're here to play a few games of golf or indulge in any number of relaxing spa treatments. Depending on where you're staying, you may not have to go far from your room.

If you're a golf lover, schedule an early-morning tee time for the famous (or infamous, depending upon the year) TPC Golf Course (480-585-4334; www.tpc.com/scottsdale), where

Quick tip: Consider reserving your spot ahead of time. You can book your tee time 90 days in advance using their online booking service.

You may also want to check out any number of Scottsdale's championship public and semiprivate courses, including the Troon North (www.troonnorthgolf.com); Legend Trail (www.legendtrailgc.com); McCormick Ranch (www.mccormickranchgolf.com); Grayhawk (www.grayhawkgolf.com); and Rancho Manana in Cave Creek (www.ranchomanana.com).

every year, golf's finest come out to play in a little game once called the Phoenix Open. (It's now called the Waste Management Open.)

If you're a spa lover, consider an Arizona-inspired treatment at the resort where you're staying or one of the area's day spas. Scottsdale spas are among the top rated in the country, and you will find plenty of choices, like an aloe vera wrap at Spa at Gainey Village (480-609-6979; www.villageclubs.com), a 50-minute jojoba and prickly pear polish at Spa at Four Seasons Resort Scottsdale (480-513-5145; www.fourseasons.com/scottsdale), or an agave body glow exfoliating treatment that begins with a full salt scrub with grapefruit essential oils and agave at the Agave Spa at Westin Kierland (480-624-1202; www.kierlandresort.com).

Late Lunch

Before you head out for an afternoon of sight-seeing, stop for a light Arizona lunch at the Daily Dose (480-994-3673; www.dailydosegrill.com). Snag a seat on the patio or find a booth inside the cool, dark interior. Get your taste buds on board for a trip through downtown Scottsdale with the Old Town Citrus Avocado Salad, rock shrimp tacos, or the green chile chicken enchiladas. Top it off with a fresh brewed desert fruit iced tea or homemade lemonade.

Afternoon Sight-Seeing

Spend the afternoon wandering the winding avenues of downtown Scottsdale. Take a one-hour, self-guided Tour through Old Town Scottsdale and check out the Native American art and jewelry, gallery-hop your way through the Marshall Way Contemporary Arts District, window-shop the boutiques throughout the Fifth Avenue Shopping District, explore the Main Street Arts

Patio seating at AZ88 on the Scottsdale Civic Center Mall

& Antiques District, or shop the Waterfront and Fashion Square Mall on Camelback.

Drinks & Appetizers

AZ/88 (480-994-5576; http://web.me .com/az88), established in 1988 by owner Karl Kopp, is an iconic Scottsdale restaurant known for its wild art, white decor, and tasty fare. The art is ever changing and unique—like the pieces of a yellow taxi cab hanging from the ceiling. It's a great Arizona stop given its proximity to Old Town Scottsdale and its place on the civic plaza, as well as its floor-to-ceiling windows/doors that open up to the huge outdoor patio. The appetizers are as unique as the art—St. Petersburg Potatoes (chips covered in smoked salmon, sour cream, cream cheese, radish, onion, and cucumber) or galettes (flatbread topped with bacon, caramelized onions, black olives, and Parmesan cheese); you'll also find standards like shrimp cocktail and hot wings.

Dinner

It's impossible to make a recommendation for good restaurants in Scottsdale, simply because there are too many choices. However, Bandera (480-994-3524; www.hillstone.com), on the corner of First Street and Scottsdale Road in Old Town, serves up gourmet cowboy chow you'll be hard pressed to find any place else in town. Now that the landmark Pink Pony restaurant is closed, someone has to take its place to serve the kind of steak Arizona is famous for (cattle is one of our five *c*'s). But that's not all they serve; the smell of chicken roasting in their giant rotisserie, which you can see through the window, is enough to pull you inside. The food is fantastic (try the mashed potatoes and steaks, and don't forget the corn bread skillet), and the service is top-notch.

After Dinner

Considered the oldest saloon in Scottsdale, the Rusty Spur (480-425-7787; www.rustyspursaloon.com) was originally built as the Farmer's State Bank in 1921. It didn't become the Rusty Spur Saloon until 1958, and it's been a Scottsdale icon ever since. Thursday through Saturday nights, passersby can hear the raucous sounds of outlaw country and classic rock played to an equally rowdy crowd as the Psychobilly Rodeo Band (www.psychobillyrodeo .com) fills this little bar with music, laughter, and a whole lot of fun. The band begins playing at 8 PM, and the place starts filling up. Don't expect to find a seat; it's often standing room only after 10 PM. But don't worry, this fun-loving crowd will move over to make room as they dance and sing along to their favorites. The band sings for tips and takes requests, so bring cash! The bar takes plastic.

DAY 2

Breakfast

The breakfast menu at The Breakfast Club (480-222-2582; www.thebreak fastclub.us) will leave you with more than the simple pancakes or eggs dilemma. Instead, you'll also have to choose between omelets and eggs Benedict or Southwestern-style eggs and flapjacks, French toast, waffles, or pancakes. Decisions, decisions, decisions . . . and that doesn't even get into the lean section of the menu, with choices like lox and Irish oatmeal or additional sides like the mouthwatering jalapeño biscuits. Needless to say, you'll be appropriately satiated and ready for a morning of shopping before you hop your plane or get in your car for your trip home.

Shopping

Part of the 730-acre master-planned Kierland Community envisioned by the locally known Herberger family and adjacent to the Westin Kierland Resort & Spa, Kierland Commons (480-348-1577; www.kierlandcommons.com) features more than 70 retail stores,

boutiques, and restaurants (both local and nationally known) in a town-square-style layout. Shops line short avenues and surround an open square with a fountain, patio-style seating, and park benches. Stores include upscale clothing and accessories at Ann Taylor LOFT, Banana Republic, and Michael Kors; home decor at Z Gallerie, Crate & Barrel, and Restoration Hardware; national favorites Victoria's Secret and Barnes & Noble; and locally owned stores like wine bar/store Bacchus Wine Made Simple (480-368-1743; www.bacchusaz.com).

Lunch Before You Go

For a quick bite before you go, try Chloe's Corner (480-998-0202; www.chloescorneraz.com). Originally owned by the homegrown restaurant group Fox Restaurant Concepts, Chloe's Corner is now owned and operated by former Fox employee and manager Ashly Young. This diner-style restaurant serves all-American favorites like grilled cheese with a twist (a three different cheese, tomato, and bacon kind of twist) or a tuna melt served on cranberry walnut bread. They also serve a soup of the day, several different salads, and sandwiches. If you're in a rush, grab your lunch from their grab 'n' go corner and take it with you!

Extend Your Stay

If you have more time, try these great places to see and things to do . . .

ARIZONA HERITAGE

Get a taste of Scottsdale's history, including information about its founder, Winfield Scott; art created by some of its earliest artists; and bits and

Shopping at Kierland Commons

Photo courtesy of Westin Kierland Resort & Spa

pieces of Scottsdale's younger days at the Scottsdale Historical Society (480-945-4499; www.scottsdalemuseum .com). The gift shop has a collection of unique Arizona children's books for sale.

Historic Old Town Scottsdale encompasses much of the 40 original acres subdivided by Rhode Island transplant Albert G. Utley in 1894. He named the city after U.S. Army chaplain Winfield Scott, who played a monumental role in encouraging the first settlers to make this their new home. The 60-minute self-guided walking tour begins at the "Little Red Schoolhouse" built in 1909, now home of the Scottsdale Historical Museum; it ends with the Scottsdale Public Library (Civic Center Branch). A total of 15 stops along the way paint a picture of this once small farming town's past,

including the Rusty Spur Saloon, originally built in 1921 as the Farmer's State Bank of Scottsdale, as well as nationally known landmarks like the Pink Pony Steakhouse (which is now closed) on Scottsdale Road. For more information on this walk, including a map and descriptions of each of the sites, visit www.scottsdalecvb.com /includes/media/docs/HistoricWalking Tour1.pdf.

Take a lunchtime tour—Tuesday through Sunday—through downtown Scottsdale with Arizona Food Tours (800-979-3370; www.arizonafood tours.com). This three-hour taste of Scottsdale leads you on a culinary trip from cowboy bar the Rusty Spur, in Old Town, to indie restaurant Cowboy Ciao, in the Marshall Way Contemporary Arts District, inviting you to delight in tasty tidbits along the way.

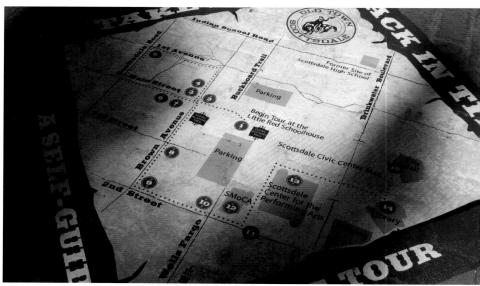

Take a self-guided walking tour of Old Town Scottsdale

ARTS & CULTURE

Take a stroll through downtown Scottsdale on any given Thursday and partake in a 30-year-old tradition—Scottsdale ArtWalk (www.scottsdale galleries.com). Home to more than one hundred galleries, Scottsdale encourages visual arts of all types, from Southwest landscapes and Native American subjects to cutting-edge contemporary. Local galleries stay open late to show off the works of various artists. Special exhibits, artists' receptions, and live music often coincide with this weekly event.

Scottsdale is home to more galleries per capita than almost any other city in the United States. The city's zest for art is mirrored by residents' votes to allocate a portion of city taxes toward the funding of public art and has made Scottsdale a prominent arts hub in the Southwest. Downtown Scottsdale is made up of five districts that meld and flow into one another, but each with a distinct personality: the

Fifth Avenue shopping district, world-renowned Marshall Way Contemporary Arts District, Main Street Arts & Antiques District, Old Town (the city's origins), and the Brown & Stetson Business District. These areas are easily navigated on foot and are peppered with specialty shops, bars, restaurants, and art galleries.

Try an early dinner at one of the area's many restaurants—perhaps Malee's on Main Street for Thai or Bandera on Scottsdale Road for gourmet Western cuisine—then take a walk through the winding avenues that make up the heart of the West's Most Western Town.

Photo courtesy of Nolan Bailey

Quick tip: For a comprehensive schedule of member galleries' schedules and individual events, including details about the weekly Scottsdale ArtWalk, visit the Scottsdale Gallery Association's Web site at www.scottsdalegalleries.com.

Frank Lloyd Wright and Taliesin West

A living monument to the life and work of architect Frank Lloyd Wright, **Taliesin West** (480-860-2700; www.franklloydwright.org)—pronounced *tally-ES-in*—is the western counterpart to Wright's home and studio Taliesin in Spring Green, Wisconsin.

In 1937, Wright began building what he considered to be his winter home as well as his personal studio and an architectural campus. What better place for Wright to showcase his unique ability to blend indoor and outdoor space than in the McDowell Mountains of the Sonoran Desert? The 550-acre property, now considered a National Historic Landmark, features a number of Wright's architectural highlights, including the Cabaret Theatre, Music Pavilion, and Seminar Theatre; Wright's private office and living quarters; the "Garden Room"; and the various terraces, walkways, gardens, and dramatic views that contribute to the magnificence of Taliesin West.

Docent-led tours cover a variety of topics about Wright and his famous property, including historical facts, architectural philosophies, and educational aspects, as well as a sight-seeing tour of the property itself.

Today Taliesin West serves as an architectural school for Wright enthusiasts. Tours are available at different times summer–fall and winter–spring; ranging from one to three hours, they highlight different aspects of the property and Wright's work.

If you like this . . . schedule a customized tour through **Ultimate Art & Cultural Tours** *(480-634-6850; www.ultimate arttours.com) and get the lowdown on not only the works of Frank Lloyd Wright, but some insight into the man himself, when their special expert takes you on a driving tour of the local buildings Wright designed, as well as a specially guided trip through Taliesin West.*

Art & Flowers in Downtown Scottsdale

Scottsdale Museum of Contemporary Art (SMoCA) (480-874-4666; www.smoca.org) was founded in 1999 as the city's only museum devoted to contemporary art, architecture, and design. The museum, originally a movie theater, was designed by award-winning architect Will Bruder; it features five galleries and a combination of permanent and changing exhibits and works. SMoCA offers the community and visitors educational programs and special events, lectures, docent-led tours, workshops, and classes.

The **Scottsdale Center for the**

Customize Your Tour

There are many ways to experience Scottsdale's arts and cultural attributes—peruse the galleries, participate in the weekly ArtWalk, and tour the museums. But what if you could meet the artist, get a personalized tour, or even create your own little piece of art? That's exactly what Ace Bailey, owner of **Ultimate Art & Cultural Tours** (480-634-6850; www.ultimatearttours.com), does for her clients: she plans customized tours that get you up close and personal with the artists and their work.

Discover the art of Navajo weaving, pottery making, or Native American jewelry making; get an expert-guided Arizona Desert Architecture Tour; take a three-gallery trip through the Scottsdale Arts District and visit with the owners, directors, and/or artists themselves, and learn firsthand about the work on display; or visit the artist's studio for an in-depth Q&A session.

Bailey has several regular tours, like the $19.56 architectural tour at Hotel Valley Ho and the free Downtown Cultural Trolley Tours given on the second Saturday of the month. To book her, visit online or call. Tours can be for one or for a group of 25.

Public art abounds in Scottsdale

Performing Arts (480-994-ARTS; www.scottsdaleperformingarts.org) features a wide variety of cultural and arts programs, including past musical performances by the likes of Joan Baez, Grammy Award winner and jazz performer Sonny Rollins, and the Glenn Miller Orchestra. Past performances include dance groups like Urban Tap and Les Grands Ballets Canadiens de Montreal; stage productions such as the Valley's longest-running play, *Late*

Scottsdale Museum of Contemporary Art

NIGHTLIFE

If there is *a* place to see and be seen in the Valley, Scottsdale is probably that place. You will find stretch Hummers pulling up to some of these nightspots; Hollywood and sports celebrities are known to party here. In Old Town, top spots like e4 (480-970-3325; 4282 N. Drinkwater Boulevard)—an award-winning venue—and Myst and the Ballroom (480-429-6000; www.mystaz.com) let you rub elbows with celebrities as you sip cocktails.

Joined by a glass catwalk, Axis /Radius (480-970-1112; www.axis -radius.com) brings you two clubs for the price of one. Dance to the high-energy beat of Radius or relax to a more mellow mix of 1970s, '80s, and '90s music at Axis. Both draw a see-and-be-seen crowd, including celebrity-status VIPs. While jeans are allowed, anything less might get you a head shake at the door. There's a cover charge of $10; free for ladies on Thursday.

Located just across the street from Axis/Radius is its sexy sister, Suede (480-970-6969; www.suedeaz.com). This sophisticated lounge and restaurant has a sleigh bed, a flaming fountain, and a selective admissions policy. Late-night menu available; reservations are a must.

The Lodge (480-945-0828; www .scottsdalelodge.com) is reminiscent of a ski lodge—a moose heads hanging on the wall, stone fireplace, take off your ski goggles kind of place. Traveling Midwesterners may somehow think they've ended up back home. The Lodge, a self-proclaimed Midwestern-style "dive bar," offers a full menu of bar-friendly appetizers, burgers, and sandwiches, as well as breakfast, and the kind of good time you won't necessarily find anywhere else in Scottsdale.

Nite Catechism; comedic performances by commentator-author David Sedaris and by the political satire group Capitol Steps; and global performances by artists like the Chinese-born pianist Yuja Wang.

Quick tip: Event times, prices, and locations vary. Events take place in Old Town Scottsdale at the Scottsdale Center for the Performing Arts Virginia G. Piper Theater and Stage 2, located at 7380 E. Second Street; Theater 4301, at the Galleria Corporate Center, on the corner of Drinkwater Boulevard and Fifth Avenue, 1 block east of Scottsdale Road; and the Amphitheater at 75th and Main streets.

In the North Scottsdale/Phoenix area, locals like to frequent Barcelona North Scottsdale (480-603-0370; 15440 Greenway-Hayden Loop, Scottsdale), a restaurant with live music and a vibrant night scene. Desert Ridge Marketplace (480-513-7586; www.shop desertridge.com; 21001 N. Tatum Boulevard, Phoenix) hosts live, local musicians in its two free outdoor venues—District Stage and AMC Fountain—on Friday and Saturday beginning at 7 PM.

For a more laid-back night, try The Comedy Spot (480-945-4422; www.thecomedyspot.net), on Third Avenue just west of Scottsdale Road. It's a small, intimate comedy club where you'll see your ticket taker opening on stage. You'll find locally and nationally known comics and have a hilariously good time. Want to brave the stage yourself? Try out for openmike night on Sunday or sign up for their comedy classes on Sunday afternoons. Reservations are recommended; call and leave your name, number, and the number of tickets you'll need, and pick them up at the door.

There are any number of fantastic indoor/outdoor bars in the downtown Scottsdale districts, especially up and down Scottsdale Road, like The Bungalow (480-994-1888; www.bungalow barandgrill.com), with its 4–7 PM happy hour and patio seating on the corner of Scottsdale Road and Stetson; Saddle Ranch Chop House (480-429-2263; www.srrestaurants.com), always good for a wild time and a ride on the famous bull; Loco Patron (480-874-0033; www.locopatron.com), with patio seating, fish tacos, and smashed potatoes; and the Salty Senorita (480-946-SALTY; www.saltysenorita.com). Several of these local restaurants have locations throughout the Valley.

OUTDOOR ADVENTURES

Scottsdale is surrounded by and encompasses thousands of acres of Sonoran Desert, mountain ranges, and natural space filled with trails, hiking paths, and flora and fauna unique to Arizona.

Biking

There are several bike paths that parallel surface streets. Indian Bend Wash is one of the most popular. Located in Scottsdale, this 10-mile paved path parallels Hayden Road from Shea Boulevard to the northern end of Tempe. The route is accessible at any point off Hayden, and there are several parking lots, including one at the northwest corner of Indian School and Hayden roads. The path is shared by every type of wheels, including bikes, in-line skates, and baby strollers.

Horseback Riding

Cave Creek Trail Rides (623-742-6700; www.cavecreektrailrides.com) offers guided horseback riding tours at Cave Creek Regional Park. One-hour rides start at about $40 per person. Two- and three-hour rides and sunset rides are available. Children under six receive complimentary pony rides; ages 6–12 get a $5 discount. The Cave Creek Regional Park can be reached by taking 32nd Street north from Carefree Highway, which is located halfway between I-17 and Scottsdale Road. There is a $5 fee to enter the park; once you're inside, follow the horse signs to the stables. Open Oct.–April.

Parks & Preserves

The 14,000 acre McDowell Sonoran Preserve (480-998-7971; www.mcdow ellsonoran.org), located in northeast Scottsdale (this is the land that Taliesin West overlooks), offers space for hik-

Bicycling in north Scottsdale

ers, bikers, climbers, and horseback riders. Several access points (including the Gateway, which features a recently built LEED-certified building and an amphitheater) and four north of Via Linda (past Frank Lloyd Wright Boulevard) connect visitors with a combination of parking, trailheads, and amenities that vary from location to location. The Gateway Loop, accessible from the Gateway Trailhead, is a scenic 4.5-mile loop with a 700-foot gain in elevation. Plan for about three hours and bring plenty of water.

Quick tip: Some of the land is designated as state land and requires a permit. For more information about the preserve, including trailheads, directions, and amenities, visit www.mcdowellsonoran.org.

Quick tip: To get to the Gateway Trailhead (18333 N. Thompson Peak Road), take the Loop 101 to Bell Road. Take Thompson Peak Road north. The trailhead is on the east side of the road.

Pinnacle Peak Park (480-312-0990; www.scottsdaleaz.gov/parks /pinnacle) is located in Scottsdale, north of the 101 where it curves west. Take the Pima Road exit, head north to Happy Valley Road, and continue east to Alma School Road past the Four Seasons Resort. Turn left at the PINNACLE PEAK PATIO RESTAURANT sign. This hike is about 3.5 miles round-trip and climbs 1,300 feet above North Scottsdale, offering an amazing view of the surrounding landscape and some of the Valley's most expensive homes. Horseback riding is allowed at the 150-acre park, but dogs and bicycles are not permitted.

The Cave Creek Regional Park (653-465-0431; www.maricopa.gov /parks/cave_creek/) campground (1.5 miles north of Carefree Highway off 32nd Street) provides campers with 38 individual "developed" sites and space for a large group, each with a parking area that can accommodate an RV up to 45 feet long, and a fire ring, in addition to the standard developed site amenities. The park provides restrooms with flush toilets and hot showers. Large groups can reserve (for a fee) the 2-acre group campground, which includes restrooms, ramadas with picnic tables, a fire ring, and an activity area. A six-unit commitment is necessary to use the facility for dry camping. The park also has 11 miles of trail and a horse staging area.

SHOPPING

In downtown Scottsdale (along Scottsdale Road between Thomas and Camelback roads), you can experience the flavor of the Old West where Scottsdale began more than one hundred years ago. What locals and tourists alike think of as Old Town is actually made up of several distinct districts. The Fifth Avenue Shopping District offers choices from shops, salons, and art galleries to nightlife and dining. The Scottsdale Arts District is home of the Thursday-night ArtWalk; this district features a mix of art from traditional to contemporary, along with craft and jewelry venues. Taken together it represents one of the largest concentrations of galleries in the United States. The Entertainment District is just that, a combination of nightclubs and restaurants. The Brown & Stetson Business District comprises a number of established businesses, hotels, restaurants, and shops. The Old Town district embodies the Old West spirit of Scottsdale with historic buildings, Western-wear shops and galleries, and jewelry, craft, and bookstores highlighting the Southwest. The Civic Center Mall features most prominently the library, Scottsdale Center for the Arts, and the Giants's spring training compound. Combined, the area offers 300-plus shops and 90 restaurants.

In addition to Kierland Commons, mentioned earlier, Scottsdale is also home to a number of shopping districts, malls, villages, and centers:

The Borgata (480-994-8048; www .westcor.com). An upscale experience of local and national specialty shops and restaurants.

Promenade Shopping Center (480-385-2820; www.pedersoninc .com). The Promenade, located at one of Scottsdale's most prominent intersections—Frank Lloyd Wright and Scottsdale Road—offers a variety of shops and restaurants.

Scottsdale Fashion Square (480-994-8048; www.westcor.com). One of the most popular shopping experiences in Scottsdale, located on the northern edge of downtown, Fashion Square features novelty shops and upscale national brands like Barneys New York.

The Shops at Gainey Village (www.theshopsgaineyvillage.com). Upscale boutiques and restaurants.

El Pedregal Shops & Dining at The Boulders Resort and Golden Door Spa (480-488-1072; www.el pedregal.com). This bilevel outdoor courtyard and its shops embody Scottsdale sophistication. Located in the shadows of The Boulders, el Pedregal features a full-service salon, boutiques, and fine and casual dining.

SPECTATOR SPORTS

The Waste Management Phoenix Open (www.phoenixopen.com), a PGA Tour event, annually draws more than 500,000 spectators. First held in 1932, the Phoenix Open, as it was originally called, failed after only three years. Under the vision and direction of Bob Goldwater Sr. and with the help of his fellow Thunderbirds, the Phoenix Open thrived again, and "the greatest show on grass" was born. This championship—one of the Valley's signature events—has raised almost

Custom Golf Tours

Serious golfers, or even leisure golfers serious about their golf, who are staying at the Millennium Resort Scottsdale may want to get in touch with Michael Luna, the resort's on-site golf concierge. Luna, author of the blog Luna's Corner (www.mill enniumhotels.com/millenniumscottsdale/golf) and golf sales manager for the resort, has created an outlet that any golfer would envy. Luna's job is developing relationships with some of the Valley's most exclusive golf properties; creating customized golf tours that include transportation, dinner, rentals, and massages; and hooking his golfers up with top-notch instructors. And he'll join you for golf, upon request. But that's not all. In addition to developing those relationships and organizing all the details, Luna is also out there vetting the courses to make sure that what he's setting up for you is a very memorable golf outing. To schedule a customized golf tour for one or for a group of golfers staying at Millennium Resort Scottsdale, you can e-mail Michael at mluna@mill-usa.com or call him at 480-367-2459.

$50 million for Arizona charities.

The Waste Management Phoenix Open is held in late January at TPC of Scottsdale. This stadium course was designed to host the Open and can accommodate the hundreds of thousands of people who attend. It does not sell out. Daily ticket admissions run about $25 per person, and prices increase to provide additional perks and advantages like access to lounges and special seating to skyboxes on the most coveted holes. This event lasts six days, with the PGA Tour the final three—Friday, Saturday, and Sunday. The Thunderbirds do an excellent job coordinating parking; access to the parking lots is convenient, and the cost of the shuttle from the parking lots to just outside the golf course is included in your ticket price. Some of the area's resorts offer great golf and accommodation packages this time of year. For accommodations close by, see *North Scottsdale* under *Pick Your Spot.*

Spring training got a little bigger in Scottsdale for the 2011 season. After decades of spring baseball in Tucson, the Cactus League's Arizona Diamond-backs (www.dbacks.com) and Colorado Rockies (http://colorado.rockies.mlb .com) have moved north to their brand new training complex at Indian Bend Road and the 101 in North Scottsdale. The only spring training facility located on Indian land, the new complex is scheduled to open in time for the 2011 spring training season.

In Old Town Scottsdale, the San Francisco Giants (480-990-7972 or 800-225-2277; www.sfgiants.com) will continue to play their spring training games at Scottsdale Stadium.

Quick tip: Finding the stadium can be tricky. Accessible from both Scottsdale and Indian School roads, the stadium is located on the northeast corner of Drinkwater Boulevard and Osborn across the street from Scottsdale Healthcare—Osborn. From the highway, take the 101 north or south to Indian School Road. Turn west onto Indian School, continue to Drinkwater Boulevard, and turn right or head north until you see the stadium.

Tempe and the East Valley

MESA, GILBERT, CHANDLER, APACHE JUNCTION, QUEEN CREEK

On the outside, it may seem you're here to visit family and friends, check out Arizona State University, or take in a spring training game or a few rounds of golf. Maybe you're here for a business trip or conference, or perhaps you've decided to make Greater Phoenix your new home. But we know why you're here. The truth is, you're looking for our fabulous weather: blue skies, a glorious sun, spectacular sunsets, and temperatures that will make your neighbors melt with envy (especially in winter—in the summer, they'll probably laugh: dry heat—ha!).

So what's the best way to enjoy all that sunshine in Tempe and its East Valley sister cities? If you're anything like I was before I traveled to Arizona, you're envisioning heated pools, towering saguaro cacti, palm trees, mountains rising up behind your hotel, and snowcapped peaks in the distance. If you've been here before, then you know that's exactly what you'll find, and you can't wait to see it again.

The East Valley is a salad bowl of academics, retirees, families, recent college grads, business professionals, business owners, and working-class individuals. You'll find that each of the cities carries a distinct personality and individual appeal—from the smart little shops in downtown Chandler to the wild, eclectic nightlife of Tempe's Mill Avenue District to the quiet old-town feel of Gilbert's main drag.

With this area as your home base, you can find any or all of the following: golfing, hiking, horseback riding, dining, spring training games, mountain biking, birding, shopping, museums, history, and both on- and off-Broadway productions. You're also close to professional basketball and baseball games, countless museums, golf courses, restaurants, nightlife, live music venues, art galleries, and boutiques in nearby Scottsdale and central Phoenix.

Pick Your Spot

Best places to stay in Tempe, and what you'll find nearby . . .

TEMPE

Chances are if you're here to visit Tempe, you'll want to stay in one of two areas: (1) Tempe and I-10: near I-10 for close proximity to South

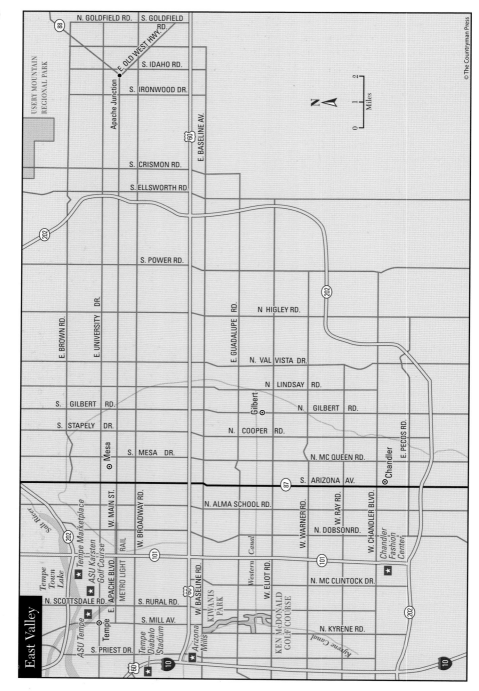

Mountain Park Preserve, Arizona Mills, and Phoenix Sky Harbor International Airport, and easy access to the rest of the Valley and Anaheim Angels spring training; or (2) Tempe and ASU: by Arizona State University's Tempe campus, with access to ASU's Sun Devil Stadium and Gammage Auditorium, Mill Avenue's shopping and dining district, Tempe Marketplace, Tempe Town Lake and Tempe Beach Park, several golf courses, Oakland A's spring training, Papago Park, Phoenix Zoo, and Desert Botanical Garden.

While there are restaurants, dining, places to go, and things to do throughout Tempe (and I'll mention a few of them), most of what you'll want to see and do can be found in one of these two areas.

I-10 in Tempe

On the west side of I-10 and adjacent to Tempe Diablo Stadium where the Anaheim Angels play their spring training games is The Buttes, A Marriott Resort (602-225-9000 or 888-867-7492; www.marriott.com), a 25-acre resort set high above the Valley. The resort features two swimming pools, lush landscaping, and spectacular views of the Valley. A winding road leads up to the resort, which has 345 rooms and 11 suites, plus tennis courts, sand volleyball, a fitness center, and a spa. It's conveniently located on the dividing line between Tempe and Phoenix,

Tempe (pronounced *tem-PEE*) was established about 1870 when Charles Trumbull Hayden settled on the banks of the Salt River and quickly built a flour mill, store, and what came to be called Hayden's Ferry to help newly settled residents traverse the waters. In 1879 Lord Darrell Duppa—the same man to suggest *Phoenix* as the name for another Valley city—stated that the area reminded him of the Vale of Tempe in Greece, and so the name was changed. In 1885 the Arizona legislature chose Tempe as the site of the Territorial Normal School. For the most part Tempe remained a small agriculturally based community until after World War II, when farms began to disappear and housing developments took their places, alongside new businesses and the ever-expanding Normal School, which became Arizona State University in 1958. Today Tempe is home to about 170,000 people. As the geographic center of the Valley of the Sun and bordered on all sides by the Valley's extensive highway system, it offers its residents prime real estate and easy access to the rest of Greater Phoenix. Visitors discover an eclectic, vibrant, cultural community of families, students, academics, and retirees with plenty to see and do, from riding a Segway along Tempe Town Lake to watching a Broadway play at Gammage Auditorium.

Water runs through the often dry bed of the Salt River after days of rain

and provides guests with an on-site spa and several dining options, including the upscale restaurant Top of the Rock (602-431-2370). The restaurant's floor-to-ceiling windows, intimate lighting, and delicious menu make for a romantic evening. Chef de Cuisine James Hildebrand consistently looks for flavors that test boundaries, such as a homemade gnocchi appetizer or a seared sea bass atop a delightful layer of varied flavors and textures. Also on-site are Tequila on the Rocks, the resort's lounge, with live music on weekends; Market Café (602-225-9000), a unique restaurant built right into the boulders that features a giant waterfall and patio seating, and serves breakfast, lunch, and dinner; and the Thirsty Cactus Pool Bar and Grill, an open-air pool bar that serves lunch (and drinks) to sunbathers.

Fast fact: Technically in Phoenix, the Desert Botanical Garden has more than 50,000 arid-land plants and 40 species of rare, threatened, or endangered plants.

Fast fact: The Segway, an innovative, electric, eco-friendly means of personal transportation, is a fun new way to experience Tempe. Segway of Tempe (623-512-2882; www.segwayoftempe.com) offers a 90-minute **Tempe Town Lake Discovery Tour.** Never been on a Segway? No worries; they provide hands-on training as part of the package.

Also located off I-10, and set back from the southwest corner of Broadway and Priest, is Fiesta Inn Conference Center (480-967-1441; www.fiestainnresort .com). This single-level property has recently renovated space, 270 rooms, and a courtyard-style pool. It offers a resort atmosphere you won't find at any of the brand hotels and extended-stay properties in this particular area.

Other hotels include Holiday Inn Express, south of Baseline on Priest, and Springhill Suites Tempe, south of the 202 and closer to the airport.

Nearby, you'll find Arizona Mills, the largest outlet mall of its kind in Arizona; Phoenix Zoo; and Desert Botanical Garden on the Tempe-Phoenix dividing line.

Also, you'll be close to Arizona State University's Tempe campus, downtown and uptown Phoenix, Chase Field, US Airways Center, and the Phoenix Convention Center, as well as Scottsdale and both the east and west parts of the Valley.

ASU in Tempe

If you're looking for resort-style accommodations close to ASU's Tempe campus, Mill Avenue, and Tempe Town Lake, Tempe Mission Palms Hotel (480-894-1400 or 800-547-8705; www.missionpalms.com) is an ideal choice. Located just off Mill Avenue, Mission Palms is within walking distance to more than a hundred restaurants, cafés, bars, stores, and boutiques, and close to several museums. A hike up "A" Mountain can start right out the front doors, and Tempe Town Lake and Tempe Beach Park are only a short walk away. You're also walking distance from ASU's Sun Devil Stadium and close to several golf

Fun fact: Guests at Mission Palms Hotel have prime seating on the rooftop deck on December 31st when Tempe celebrates the coming New Year with fireworks over Tempe Town Lake. (Book early; they often sell out months in advance.)

Tempe Center for the Arts

courses, including ASU Karsten Golf Course, as well as Tempe Center for the Arts, Phoenix Zoo, and Desert Botanical Garden.

The hotel features a lush courtyard setting, rooftop deck with panoramic views, an outdoor heated swimming pool, fitness center, tennis court, and basketball hoop. Enjoy the abundant breakfast buffet available on weekends at Mission Grille or have a drink at Harry's Place. The recently renovated 300-plus rooms offer high-speed Internet access and top-notch service.

Only blocks away from ASU's Tempe campus, this area is served by the city's free shuttle, FLASH (www.tempe.gov/tim/bus/flash.htm), that serves the Tempe campus and downtown Tempe every 10 minutes Monday–Friday. You can pick up FLASH right on Mill and take it up and down Mill Avenue or to ASU. Mission Palms is also a short walk from the METRO Light Rail (www.valleymetro .org/metro_light_rail) station at Rio Salado and Mill Avenue; this provides access west to downtown Phoenix and Sky Harbor International Airport or east to Mesa and numerous attractions along the way. Buy an all-day pass for $5 and hop on and off the rail at your leisure.

For an ASU, family-friendly location, try Four Points by Sheraton Tempe (480-968-3451; www.fourpointstempe.com), on Rural Road just south of Apache Avenue and a short walk from Barrett Honor College on the southeast edge of campus. A brand new hotel, Four Points is close to the light rail stations at University and Rural (0.5 mile) and Dorsey and Apache (0.7 mile).

The hotel offers quite a few free amenities: daily deluxe breakfast, bottled water (a welcome perk in Arizona), shuttle service with a 5-mile radius, daily paper, and Wi-Fi. You'll also find three dining options, including a snack bar and full restaurant with limited hours for breakfast, lunch, and dinner.

If you're an on-the-go kind of guest who plans to spend little time in your hotel room, consider staying at Aloft Tempe (480-621-3303; www.alofttempe .com). This European-style hotel offers small, comfortable rooms to spend your nights. Strategically located within a mile of ASU, Tempe Marketplace, downtown Tempe, and countless other locations, it offers an accessible home base just south of the Loop 202. Aloft features an on-site, make-it-yourself snacks and coffee drinks bar all day and a minilounge open in the evenings. Check-in by kiosk, take

Aloft Tempe is a trendy boutique hotel

the colorfully lighted elevator up to your room, and settle your things before you head back out. You'll also find a courtyard-style pool off the lobby, a pool table in the lounge, and free Wi-Fi at this energetic little hotel.

Adjacent to ASU's Tempe campus on Apache Avenue between Mill Avenue and Rural Road, Twin Palms Hotel (800-367-0835; www.twinpalmshotel.com) is a seven-story high-rise hotel with an International House of Pancakes (IHOP) located on property. The 139 rooms feature sliding glass doors, satellite TV, and 24-hour room service. Complimentary access to ASU's Recreation Complex and its three Olympic-sized pools, fitness equipment, and aerobics classes. The hotel offers an excellent location for parents and students visiting campus.

EAST VALLEY

Elsewhere in the East Valley, you'll find a number of extended-stay properties, inexpensive hotels, and RV parks in Mesa; the historic San Marcos property in Chandler; and Gold Canyon Golf Resort in Apache Junction.

In the city of Mesa, home of the Chicago Cubs in spring, you'll find more than 60 hotels, motels, and resorts varying in amenities from first-class, full-service properties to cozy inns and RV parks. Hotel brands include Residence Inn and Courtyard by Marriott, La Quinta Inn & Suites, Holiday Inn Hotel & Suites, Days Inn, and Best Western.

For an excellent centrally located hotel in Mesa, consider the Phoenix Marriott Mesa (480-898-8300; www.marriott.com), strategically set just off Main Street. Adjacent to the Mesa Convention Center and within walking distance of the Mesa Public Library, the recently renovated Phoenix Marriott Mesa offers guests 275 rooms, a heated pool, a spa, and a fitness center. Downtown Mesa (with several museums, including the fabulous Mesa Art Center) and Hohokam Stadium (where the Cubs currently play their spring training games) are only minutes away.

Gold Canyon Golf Resort (480-671-5546 or 800-624-6445; www.gcgr.com), at the foot of the Superstition Mountains, offers guests casitas, championship golf, a fitness center, and a full-service spa. There are three on-site dining options, Internet access, and golf packages available.

The City of Chandler has successfully introduced two very attractive elements to Arizona tourism: downtown Chandler, with its live music concerts and plays, local restaurants, art galleries, boutiques, and weekly art walk; and Chandler Fashion Center, with a number of well-known restaurant chains and stores, including Cheesecake Factory, Barnes & Noble, Williams-Sonoma, and Pottery Barn.

Located in the heart of downtown Chandler is the Valley's first resort. The Crowne Plaza San Marcos Golf Resort (480-812-0900 or 800-528-8071; www.san marcosresort.com) boasts 295 rooms, an 18-hole golf course, tennis courts, two heated pools, two Jacuzzis, a fitness center, two restaurants, and a lounge. Recently renovated, it is within walking distance of a number of excellent local restaurants, shops, and boutiques, such as El Zocalo Mexican Grille, Murphy's Law Irish Pub, Kokopelli Winery, and San Tan Brewery.

Public art in downtown Mesa

Gilbert

Liberty Market (480-892-1900; www
.libertymarket.com) in downtown
Gilbert offers a combination of grilled
paninis, gourmet salads, and pastas for
lunch and dinner, and an eclectic
breakfast menu that includes scrambled eggs, breakfast quesadillas, and
grilled bread pudding.

Joe's Real BBQ (480-503-3805;
www.joesrealbbq.com), owned by the
same Joe who owns Liberty Market
and Joe's Farm Grill (480-JOE-GRIL;
www.joesfarmgrill.com), all in Gilbert,
serves delicious barbecued beef, chick-
en, pork—you name it, and they barbecue it. Joe's serves its barbecued goods
cafeteria style: get in line, order from
the big menu board, and grab your
food. You'll find old-fashioned sodas
(like 7UP in a bottle!) and Joe's own
homemade root beer; the biggest potatoes you've ever seen (get them heaped
with everything you can think of,
including meat); and homemade

Joe's Real BBQ

desserts including cookies, cakes, and
brownies.

Queen Creek

Tour Arizona's own olive mill—the
Queen Creek Olive Mill (480-888-
9290; www.queencreekolivemill.com).
This family-owned business grows and
presses olives for the production of
extra-virgin olive oil. Arizona's climate
makes for ideal growing conditions and
an extended season. Tours (including
an opportunity to taste-test) are available daily; there's also a shop where
you can sample the olive oils and other
treats, and a little on-site restaurant,
del Piero, where you can enjoy breakfast or lunch.

INDEPENDENT COFFEEHOUSES

Tempe

Maybe it's all of the college students
cramming for exams or all of the
retirees unable to kick the habit. Whatever the reason, Tempe's not that big,
but it seems to have more than its fair
share of independent coffee shops.

*If you like this . . . check out
www.arizona-coffee.com for the latest
and greatest on Arizona's independent
coffeehouses.*

Gold Bar Espresso (480-839-
3082; www.goldbarespresso.com), on
the northeast corner of McClintock
and Southern, features Allan Brothers
coffee, baked treats, free Wi-Fi, and a
warm, welcoming atmosphere that has
locals stopping in on a regular basis for
their coffee and a conversation. They
feature live jazz on weekends; they're
open early (6 AM) and stay open late
(11 PM). On the opposite corner is
Xtreme Bean Coffee Company (480-
820-0333; 1707 E. Southern Avenue),
they also have early/late hours, and to

Solo Café is one of Tempe's many indie coffeehouses

accommodate the college crowd, they're open 5 AM Friday through 11 PM Sunday.

Solo Café (480-838-7656; 107 E. Baseline Road), at Mill Avenue and Baseline, resembles someone's private study, with plenty of comfy seating (both indoor and out), floor-to-ceiling bookshelves, free Wi-Fi, and a laundry list of great teas, coffees, and espressos.

Steve's Espresso (480-777-5373; www.stevesespresso.com), on McClintock south of Baseline, serves French press coffee as standard fare and offers plenty of iced, frozen, and hot variations of the coffee bean, plus a number of loose leaf teas, steeped to perfection in a cast iron teapot.

Bunna Coffee & Tea (480-377-2886; www.bunnacoffee.com), located on the northwest corner of Elliot and Rural roads, prides itself on being an organic, free trade coffee shop. They serve a delicious menu of baked goods, breakfast and lunch wraps and paninis, plus a whole list of coffees and loose leaf teas.

West of McClintock on the north side of Broadway is one of the newest additions to Tempe's coffee haven—Cartel Coffee Lab (480-225-3899;

www.cartelcoffeelab.com) is located near ASU's Tempe Campus; some say it's the best coffee in town. Second location in downtown Phoenix.

ASU in Tempe

During the week, check out Romancing the Bean (480-921-4077; www.romancingthebean.com). Located along Tempe Town Lake in the Hayden Ferry Lakeside building, they're open for breakfast, lunch, or coffee, or an immensely gratifying dessert from their delicious pastry case.

Quick tip: They're super busy for lunch hour but tend to quiet down once the business crowd heads back to their offices.

Chandler

East Valley favorite Coffee Rush (480-507-0930; www.coffeerushcafe.com) has a shop each in Gilbert and Chandler.

Mesa

Inside the Bungalow (480-844-2353; www.insidethebungalow.com) is in downtown Mesa, and Into the Bean Coffee House (480-890-0579; www .intothebean.com) is across the street from Mesa Community College on Southern in Mesa.

Gilbert

Liberty Market (480 892 1900; www .libertymarket.com), on Gilbert Road in downtown Gilbert, serves breakfast, lunch, and dinner, and boasts a full espresso bar that features drinks as dessert, like the cortadito, a Cuban microlatte, and the Ca Phe, an iced Vietnamese coffee.

PIZZA

Pizza and *desert* may not be the first connection you'd make, but the Valley is a haven for transplants from New York City and Chicago—and they brought with them their love of pizza. The Valley has a number of well-known ('round these parts anyway) pizza parlors. Two in particular seem to rival each other for most popular in town: local chain Oregano's and world-renowned Pizzeria Bianco. However, each of these spots has its faithful followers. After all, each turns out first-class pizza.

> **If you like this . . .** *try the world-famous Pizzeria Bianco in downtown Phoenix at Heritage Square or Grimaldi's in Old Town Scottsdale.*

Tempe

While world-famous Pizzeria Bianco in Phoenix embodies the spirit of its chef, Oregano's Pizza Bistro (480-858-0501; www.oreganos.com) embodies the spirit of its "founder," Lawrence of Oregano. Though Lawrence never saw the pizzeria that bears his nickname, his essence has infused the restaurant with the ingredients that keep folks coming back again and

Quick tip: Be prepared to wait in line. It may only be pizza, but it's among the best you'll ever have.

Quick tip: There are several Oregano's locations in the East Valley: Tempe, on University west of ASU; Mesa, at Dobson and Southern; and Gilbert, on Gilbert Road.

again—Chicago-style pizzas, family, and fun. Be prepared for a wait—over an hour is not unheard of and, depending on day and time, often the norm. Still, with big-band music, drinks from the bar, and the occasional garlic bread treat making the rounds, this place makes waiting fun. And the pizza is delish! Known for deep-dish pizzas, Oregano's offers myriad toppings as well as gourmet thin-crust pizzas, traditional spaghetti (loved by many), and a stack of other choices, including sandwiches and salads so big you'll need to share with your neighbors the next table over. And despite the pizza, great frozen Bellinis (sparkling wine and peach puree), and appetizers, you need to save room for dessert—a *huge* chocolate or macadamia nut cookie topped with vanilla ice cream. It might be the best dessert in town!

Nello's (480-897-2060; www .nellosscottsdale.com), a Valley institution, has great salads to complement their pizzas.

Rosati's (480-820-4444; www .rosatispizza.com) cooks up perhaps the best Chicago-style thin-crust pizza in town.

Mesa

Organ Stop Pizza (480-813-5700; www.organstoppizza.com) is a local favorite and home to one of the world's largest Wurlitzer theater organs.

48 Hours

If you don't have much time to spend here, or if you've only allocated a couple of days of your vacation to the East Valley, this short-trip itinerary will give you an idea of what to do while you're here. While two days is not enough time to do everything here, it's plenty of time catch some of the best of what the area offers.

GETTING THERE

After checking into your hotel, check out what's happening in the Mill Avenue District. If you're staying at the Mission Palms, just walk out the lobby doors and take a right on Fifth Street. If you're staying elsewhere, head to Mill Avenue and find a parking spot. Street parking is metered (but not on weekends and evenings); you can also try the parking lot off Maple Avenue (just west of Mill) and Fifth Street.

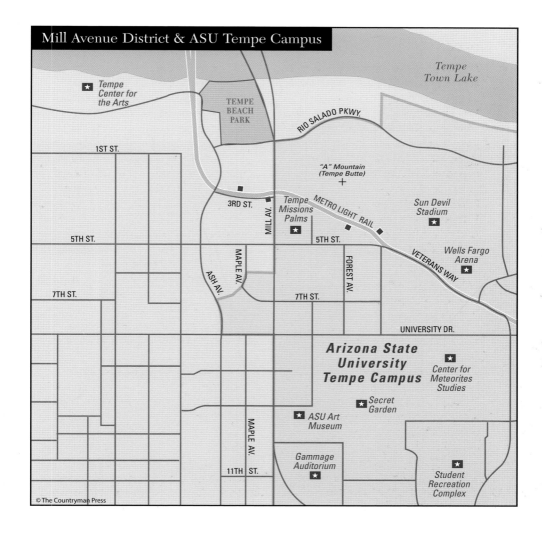

Mill Avenue District & ASU Tempe Campus

Tempe Town Lake

Tempe Center for the Arts

TEMPE BEACH PARK

RIO SALADO PKWY.

1ST ST.

"A" Mountain (Tempe Butte)

3RD ST.

MILL AV.

Tempe Missions Palms

METRO LIGHT RAIL

Sun Devil Stadium

5TH ST.

5TH ST.

ASH AV.

MAPLE AV.

Wells Fargo Arena

VETERANS WAY

7TH ST.

7TH ST.

FOREST AV.

UNIVERSITY DR.

Arizona State University Tempe Campus

Center for Meteorites Studies

Secret Garden

MAPLE AV.

ASU Art Museum

Gammage Auditorium

11TH ST.

Student Recreation Complex

© The Countryman Press

There's a cost to park, but getting your ticket validated reduces the expense. You can also take the light rail and get off at the Downtown Tempe/Tempe Town Lake exit.

There are numerous restaurants, bars, and cafés located up and down Mill Avenue and hidden on adjacent streets. For drinks and appetizers, consider a margarita or Dos Equis at Macayo's Depot Cantina (480-966-6677; www.depotcantina.com), on Ash Avenue north of Fifth Avenue. An Arizona original, the Depot is a 20-year-old Tempe tradition with a large shaded outdoor patio and bar. Inside the restaurant, walls are covered in colorful murals. Chips and salsa are the standard; complement them with an order of minichimis or a Baja pizza.

Fun fact: The original Macayo's opened at 4001 N. Central in Phoenix in 1952. It's still open, and today it's located along the METRO Light Rail route. Find out more in the "Phoenix" chapter.

For dinner, Monti's is a must. The longest occupied space in Tempe, Monti's La Casa Vieja (480-967-7594; www.montis.com) was originally the home of Tempe founder Charles Trumbull Hayden and the birthplace of U.S. senator Carl Hayden. More than 130 years old, the ancient adobe building is a charming hodgepodge of individual rooms connected by winding (and somewhat confusing) corridors.

Macayo's Depot Cantina in Tempe

Making your way among the various rooms is like wandering through a maze. If you get lost on your way to the bathroom, just ask one of the friendly waitstaff to lead you back.

Located on the southwest corner of Mill Avenue and First Street, the original home was built by the elder Hayden in 1871. "The Old House"—as the Hayden family called the original adobe structure and the namesake for its current name—was purchased in 1954 by Leonard F. Monti Sr. as a restaurant. Since then Monti's has dazzled locals and visitors alike with its steaks, seafood, and homemade desserts, and serves half a million meals a year. Beware their famous "Roman" bread. Despite the fact that it's delicious, you'll want to save room for the rest of their fabulous menu (try the Arizona-raised beef, the Full Monti Burger, or Monti's Signature Salad, with house-made Roquefort dressing).

After dinner, depending upon your style and tastes, you may want to catch an unconventional and irreverent off-, off-, off-Broadway production by Stray Cat Theatre (480-820-8022; www.stray cattheatre.org). The group affords local playwrights, actors, and artists an

opportunity to showcase their talents before a live audience. It's a shocking, if titillating, experience, with productions like the *Play about the Naked Guy* and the very gory *12th Night of the Living Dead* (beware the front row; it's considered a "splash zone"). Plays are shown at Tempe Center for the Performing Arts, just off Mill Avenue on Sixth Street.

If you like this . . . but you're looking for a family-friendly theater experience, check out **Childsplay** *(480-350-2822; www.childsplayaz.org), which performs at Tempe Center for the Arts.*

Other options include taking a stroll down the street-level staircase on the corner of Fifth and Mill to The Big Bang (480-557-5595; 501 S. Mill) and its dueling pianos for a fun and raucous evening of music and laughter, or trying the very inexpensive reverse happy hour at Dave's Electric Brew Pub (480-967-5353; www.daveselectric brewpub.com), east of Mill on College Avenue and Veteran's Way (a light rail stop). Off Mill, you'll find the Tempe IMPROV (480-921-9877; 930 E. University Drive, Suite D1): It's big, it's famous, and it serves a kind of dinner. Expect nationally known comics and a hilariously good time.

DAY 1

Take a Hike
If you're here to enjoy the outdoors, a hike should be on your to-do list. Located where it is, in the midst of everything and very nearly at the center of the Valley, Tempe offers easy access to any number of hiking spots. Earlier is better, as the sun and heat

gain intensity throughout the day. Grab a quick breakfast and plenty of water, and a healthy snack if you plan to be out long. If you want a quick, steep hike, try "A" Mountain. Also known as Hayden Butte or Tempe Butte, it's right off Mill Avenue, and if you're staying down that way, it's practically in your hotel's backyard. The trail is fairly steep, but short. You can get to it via the trailhead, accessible behind the Veteran's Way light rail stop at the end of College Avenue.

If you like this . . . try Piestewa Peak, off US 51 north of the Biltmore area in Phoenix. Like "A" Mountain, it's another very steep, but short, hike. You'll get a great workout on the old glutes. But it's not for beginners.

If you want a longer hike or some space to run, mountain bike, or go horseback riding among the cacti,

Did you know? The *A* on "A" Mountain should be a bright yellow in honor of Arizona State University's school colors. There's another "A" Mountain in Tucson, painted to represent the University of Arizona's colors. Students from the rival schools have been known to paint the opposing school's *A* the wrong color.

you'll want to block out your morning for a trip to South Mountain Park Preserve (www.phoenix.gov/PARKS/hike soth.html). With more than 16,000 acres of space to roam, it's the largest urban park in the United States. It's a short drive to one of the entrances. Trails range from easy to hard and range from 0.8 mile to more than 20 miles. With more than 60 miles of trails

"A" Mountain is a Tempe landmark

to choose from, you're sure to find one to meet your needs. (For more information, see the *Outdoor Adventures* section in the "Phoenix" chapter.)

If you like this . . . try another a longer hike on the back side of Camelback Mountain at Camelback Road on the Scottsdale-Phoenix border. This is not the Echo Canyon entrance, which is overcrowded and for the über-adventurer. Plus, it's impossible to find parking, especially on weekends.

Stop for Lunch

Irish food is not exactly the kind of food Arizona brings to mind, but St. Patrick's Day is a pretty big deal here, so it's only natural that we have our share of excellent Irish pubs. Rúla Búla (480-929-9500; www.rulabula .com), on Mill Avenue adjacent to Mission Palms, is one of our favorites. It's been named best Irish pub in town by several local media outlets. Aptly named, Rúla Búla—taken from a Gaelic saying meaning "uproar and commotion"—provides a rowdy good time; just what the owners were aiming for. You'll find live Irish entertainment in the evenings, but for lunch it's fairly quiet, though often busy. The excellent Irish menu has so many delicious options that you will have a hard time choosing. But the dishes are large enough to share, so keep that in mind when you're deciding between the best

---

Fun fact: The Phoenix St. Patrick's Day Parade that takes place on Third Street in central Phoenix started in 1984 and now draws some 50,000 spectators each year.

Quick tip: Sit outside on the patio for an outdoor Arizona experience.

---

fish-and-chips in town, the incredible shepherd's pie, and one of several mouthwatering salads—and that's *if* you haven't already stuffed yourself on the Irish soda bread they bring to your table and that glass of Guinness you ordered first.

If you like this . . . try D'Arcy McGee's in the District at Tempe Marketplace (by the movie theater) or Murphy's Law in Chandler. Also try the Turf Accountant on Central Avenue in the Roosevelt District or Seamus McCaffrey's at Central Avenue and Monroe in downtown Phoenix, or the Skeptical Chymist in North Scottsdale.

Afternoon Sight-Seeing

If you like art, take a couple of hours to wander through the ASU Art Museum (480-965-2787; http://asuartmuseum .asu.edu), located on Mill Avenue. The museum is free to visitors and features two separate spaces—the Nelson Fine Arts Center and Ceramics Research Center—with more than 12,000 objects. Together, the centers offer almost 60,000 square feet of contemporary art and ceramics from all over the world. The museum features an eclectic collection of contemporary work from a diverse group of artists, including those using new and unique methods of presentation, contemporary Latin American pieces, and art of the Southwest. Named "the single most impressive venue for contemporary art in Arizona" by *Art in America* magazine, the museum holds more than 10,000 pieces, with almost 50,000 square feet of space in five galleries. It's on the east side of Mill Avenue, just north of Gammage Auditorium. You'll find innovative productions like Canadian artist Jillian Mcdonald's video installation *Zombies vs. Vampires* as well as more traditional pieces.

Extend Your Stay

If you have more time, try these great places to see and things to do . . .

ARIZONA HERITAGE

At the Chandler Museum (480-782-2717; www.chandlermuseum.org), you'll find artifacts of prehistoric Southwestern Native Americans, photographs, and a replica of Chandler's first store in this tribute to Chandler and central Arizona. Find it in Chandler at Arizona Avenue and Buffalo Street, a block south of Chandler Boulevard or a block north of Boston Street.

Located in downtown Mesa 1 block north of Main Street, the Arizona Museum of Natural History (480-644-2230; www.azmnh.org) was a mere 3,000 square feet when in opened in 1977; today it is an 80,000-square-foot facility that features a variety of exhibits illustrating Southwestern natural and cultural history. Often called "the dinosaur museum" by local children, the Arizona Museum of Natural History features the largest collection of dinosaur bones in the state.

Petersen House Museum (480-350-5151; www.tempe.gov/petersen house), built in 1892, is one of the few remaining historic homes in the Valley representing the Victorian architectural era. It was the home of Niels Petersen, a businessman, community leader, and rancher who arrived in Tempe in 1871. His sprawling 160-acre ranch stretched from what is now Southern Avenue north to Alameda Street, and from I-10 east to Priest Drive. The Petersen House, donated in 1979 to the city of Tempe, stands at the northwest corner of Priest and Southern. The home, with its 12-foot ceilings, gables, porches, balconies, and restored period furnishings, continues to be an excellent reflection of period architecture.

The recently renovated Tempe History Museum (480-350-5100; www.tempe.gov/museum) invites you to take a stroll through this interactive tribute to Tempe's history. The muse-

Tempe History Museum

Arizona State University (480-965-9011; www.asu.edu) has expanded incredibly since its start as the Arizona Normal School in Tempe in 1885. With only 20 women and 13 men in its first graduating class, ASU has grown to a major university offering more than 250 undergraduate degrees, master's degrees, doctoral and terminal programs, online programs and a law degree program to almost 60,000 students on four campuses throughout the Valley: the 700-acre Tempe Campus in downtown Tempe, ASU West at 47th Avenue, and Thunderbird in the West Valley, ASU Polytechnic School in Mesa, and the newest—Downtown Phoenix Campus—n downtown Phoenix. ASU offers a variety of credit, noncredit, evening, weekend, and alternative-delivery-style courses to accommodate working students, as well as traditional-style classes for full-time learners. It also offers a variety of events, programs, and resources that are open to the public, many of them free, including exhibits at Nelson Fine Arts Center, the ASU Planetarium, and a 3.2-million-volume library system.

ASU's Main Campus, Tempe

um is on the southwest corner of Rural and Southern, at the Tempe Public Library campus.

ARTS & CULTURE

Museums & Galleries

There are more than 20 museums and galleries on ASU's Tempe campus, and they're all *free*. For a complete list that includes hours and locations, check here: www.asu.edu/museums. For a map, visit http://museums.asu.edu /museums_map. The collection of museums and exhibits spans fine arts, history and culture, and natural sciences, and includes the Archeological Research Institute, Museum of Anthropology, and the R.S. Dietz Museum of Geology.

Explore space via the School of Earth and Space Exploration's many facilities, including the CMS Meteorite Museum; the Space Photography Lab (SPL), which features images and maps from every major U.S. spacecraft mission; Planetarium; or the Mars Space Flight Facility—to name a few. To take a walking tour of the sites, download a map at http://sese.asu.edu/files/documents/SESE_Walking_Tour_Map.jpg.

Wander the many galleries on ASU's Tempe campus; you'll find fine-art pieces in more than 10 galleries and museums across campus, featuring works of art by national, international, and local artists, including ASU students, faculty, and staff.

If you like this . . . try the Phoenix Art Museum in uptown Phoenix. From Tempe, take the light rail to Central Avenue and McDowell Road. Or, visit the Heard Museum (Native American art), a little farther up Central Avenue at Encanto Boulevard.

Mesa Contemporary Arts (480-644-6500; www.mesaartscenter.com) at Mesa Arts Center, has been a part of the Mesa art scene since 1976, and has presented exhibits of art by both emerging and internationally recognized contemporary artists. Its varying exhibits and works make up the five-gallery, subterranean visual arts compound within the Mesa Arts Center (at the southeast corner of Main and Center streets). The North Gallery specifically features local artists from the Greater Phoenix area .

If you like this . . . try the Phoenix Art Museum in central Phoenix or the West Valley Art Museum in Surprise.

Theater
Check out the Tempe Center for the Arts (480-350-2829; www.tempe.gov/tca), located on Rio Salado Parkway at the western edge of Tempe Town Lake, for live music, plays, and events, including the family-friendly Childsplay productions; the Lakeshore Jazz Series; and the art gallery, which features special exhibits.

Mesa Contemporary Arts

Tempe Center for the Arts

Gammage Auditorium (480-965-5062; www.asugammage.com), which seats more than three thousand patrons, was the last design of nationally known architect Frank Lloyd Wright. The building, well known in the Tempe area for its resemblance to a tiered wedding cake, is acoustically sound and hosts concerts, theater, film, dance, and special events year-round. Tickets can be ordered online at www.ticketmaster.com or at www.asugammage.com.

The Mesa Arts Center (480-644-6500; www.mesaartscenter.com) boasts 212,755 square feet of space, making it the largest and most comprehensive arts center in Arizona. Home to visual and the performing arts as well as an educational venue, the center is located in the center of downtown Mesa at the southeast corner of Main and Center streets. It utilizes four state-of-the-art and outdoor entertainment areas to bring a variety of live performances to the East Valley. Events range from country music star Vince Gill to the world-renowned Vienna Choir Boys, hometown favorites like the Mesa Symphony Orchestra, off-Broadway shows including *Fully Committed*, the ballet, Shakespearean plays, and Broadway shows like *Cats*. Program schedules and tickets are available online. The box office is open Monday–Saturday 10–5, Sunday noon–4, and two hours prior to showtimes.

Biking

Voted the best bike store in the Valley, Tempe Bicycle (480-966-6896; www .tempebicycle.com) has served Valley residents and tourists for more than 30 years. Owners Bud and Yvonne Morrison are passionate bicyclists. Together with their well-trained staff, they can help you find a new bike and accessories, or rent a road bike or mountain bike. Bikes are available for half- and full-day rental, or for several days at a time. There is also the option to purchase your rental bike.

Tempe boasts more than 150 miles of dedicated bikeway—not to mention the Silver Level Bicycle Friendly Community Award, given by the League of American Bicyclists to only 13 other communities in the United States. Bikeways connect various sections of town, including Arizona State University's Tempe Campus, Tempe Town Lake, and Papago Park in Phoenix. Surrounding Tempe Town Lake are 5 miles of paths for bicycling, jogging, or in-line skating. The paths connect to the historic Tempe Beach Park. Originally built in 1931, this 25-acre park was completely renovated in 1999 as part of the construction of the Town Lake.

Parks

Papago Park (www.phoenix.gov/PARKS/hikpagud .html) is a popular site located on the border of Phoenix and Tempe. The park is home to the Phoenix Zoo and Desert Botanical Garden. Its central location and easy paths with little or no elevation change make it a popular hiking and biking choice. To hike around Papago Buttes, park on W. Park Drive, and to explore the famous Hole in the Rock—a natural opening in the red-rock butte—park just past the zoo at the information center. Park trails range from 0.1 mile (Hole-in-the-Rock Trail) to 4 miles (West Park Loop Trail).

The Usery Mountain Recreation Area (480-984-0032; www.maricopa .gov/parks/usery), in the southeast part of the Valley, is 12 miles northeast of Mesa and offers campsites, numerous hiking and horseback-riding trails, as well as an archery range. Some of the spaces at the Buckhorn Family Campground are handicapped accessible. Farther east is the Lost Dutchman State Park (480-982-4485; http://az stateparks.com/Parks/LODU/index .html), in the Superstition Mountains, with additional campsites and hiking trails.

Rock Climbing

Phoenix Rock Gym (480-921-8322; www.phoenixrockgym.com), located in Tempe, offers an indoor rock-climbing experience for beginners as well as intermediate- and lead-level climbers. With 30-foot walls and 15,000 square feet of climbing space (including a bouldering area), it's a fun and invigorating experience. Show up and sign a waiver; you can rent equipment or bring your own. If you're new to climbing, don't worry: you get a quick but thorough review first.

Water Sports

Tempe Town Lake, located just north of the Mill Avenue District and Arizona State University, is a 220-acre urban lake, the largest in the United States. It's a great spot for boating, kayaking, and fishing. Visitors can rent boats and kayaks at the marina on the lake or try something a little more wild—tubin' down the Salt River. Contact Salt River Tubing & Recreation, Inc. (480-984-3305; www.saltrivertub ing.com) or Desert Voyagers Guided Raft Trips (480-998-7238;

www.desertvoyagers.com) for more information about this favorite local summer activity.

SHOPPING

Tempe Marketplace (480-966-9338; www.tempemarketplace.com) is one of the Valley's latest outdoor shopping and dining experiences. Located where the 202 and 101 intersect, along the south edge of Tempe Town Lake, this very cool space takes shopping to a new level. A combination of shops and restaurants front an open-air common area complete with misters, palm trees, fountains, fireplaces, tables, chairs, couches, and umbrellas, inviting you to hang out and enjoy the Arizona weather. Other such spots include San Tan Village (www.shopsantanvillage.com) in southeast Mesa and Dana Park Village Square (www.danapark.com) in Mesa, just off US 60.

If you like this . . . try Desert Ridge Marketplace or Kierland Commons in north Phoenix, or Biltmore Fashion Park in the Phoenix Biltmore District.

Among the East Valley's more traditional malls is Arizona Mills (480-491-9700; www.simon.com/Mall/?id =1226), located at I-10 and US 60 in Tempe. It is the state's largest value and entertainment megamall and features more than 175 manufacturers' outlets, restaurants, and entertainment venues, including the 24-theater Harkins Cinema; an IMAX theater boasting a six story, 120-foot-wide screen; and GameWorks, a high-tech entertainment facility with a variety of virtual-reality games and vintage video games like PacMan, Tetris, and Donkey Kong.

Chandler Fashion Center (480-812-8488; www.westcor.com), off Loop 101 in Chandler, is the East Valley's

Mill Avenue District

newest mall and, on weekends especially, still reels from the convergence of locals starving for a shopping mecca close to home. You'll find a number of high-end stores, like Nordstrom, Williams-Sonoma, and Pottery Barn, as well as standard choices such as Gap and Baby Gap, a variety of popular chain restaurants like P. F. Chang's and the Cheesecake Factory, and a great theater.

For mall shopping in Mesa, check out Fiesta Mall (480-833-4121; www .shopfiesta.com) and Superstition Springs Center (480-832-0212; www .superstitionsprings.com).

The Mill Avenue District (www .downtowntempe.com) is located in downtown Tempe close to Tempe Town Lake and Arizona State University's Main Campus, featuring more than a hundred shops, restaurants, and bars. Restaurant experiences include local favorites Monti's La Casa Vieja, Caffé Boa, House of Tricks, Rúla Búla Irish Pub, and national/regional chains like Fatburger, the Last Great Hamburger Stand, Z'Tejas Southwestern Grill (for the best frozen Chambord margaritas), and Hooters. You will also find an energetic nightlife teeming with all age groups.

Tempe's Changing Hands Bookstore (480-730-0205; www.changing hands.com) is a local favorite. Adjacent to another local favorite, the Wildflower Bread Company (480-838-9773; www.wildflowerbread.com), which serves gourmet sandwiches and salads, Changing Hands celebrates local and national authors with weekly and daily events as well as monthly book signings by some of today's most popular authors.

With the Crowne Plaza San Marcos Golf Resort as downtown Chandler's main focal point, the area has been restored to a vibrant shopping

Caffé Boa

and dining district. You will find great restaurants, including La Stalla Cucina Rustica (480-855-9990; 68 W. Buffalo Street), an Italian eatery located across from the historic San Marcos Resort, and Serrano's Mexican Restaurant (480-899-3318; 141 S. Arizona Avenue), a local favorite that serves great Mexican food at a fair price; this is their original location. You will also find a variety of alluring shops, boutiques, and art galleries among the wine bars and restaurants.

SPORTS SCENE

Golf
Named after Karsten Solheim, the founder of the Ping Golf Company, ASU Karsten Golf Course (480-921-8070) is located close to Arizona State University's Tempe Campus. Dobson

Ranch Golf Course (480-644-2291) is an 18-hole championship course in Mesa that offers an inexpensive golf experience. Ocotillo Golf Resort (480-917-6660; www.ocotillogolf.com), in Chandler, is very popular with the locals and well known for its water features. Three nine-hole courses can be combined to create three separate 18-hole courses.

Spectator Sports

Watch the Anaheim Angels (888-994-2567; www.angelsbaseball.com) play in spring at Tempe Diablo Stadium. Tempe has hosted the Anaheim Angels since 1993. Ticket prices start as low as $5 and are available on-site or online. The complex includes six and a half practice fields in addition to the main stadium, which was dedicated as Gene Autry Field in 1999 in honor of the for-

mer Angels's owner who passed away after the 1998 season.

Cheer on the Chicago Cubs (800-905-3315; www.cubs.com), who played the 2010 season at Hohokam Stadium, in Mesa. Ticket prices range from $5 to $15 and can be purchased on-site or online; wheelchair-accessible seating is available.

ASU Athletics (480-965-2381; www.asu.edu) Pac-10 sports take place between August and May. The Insight Bowl (480-350-0911; www.insight bowl.com), an NCAA football game, occurs in December, and the Fiesta Bowl (480-350-0911; www.tostitos fiestabowl.com), now at University of Phoenix Stadium in Glendale, typically falls in late December or early January. See "Glendale and the West Valley" for more information about University of Phoenix Stadium.

4

Glendale and the West Valley

SURPRISE, LITCHFIELD, GOODYEAR, THE SUN CITIES

The West Valley, which makes up the western portion of the Greater Phoenix metropolitan area or Valley of the Sun, comprises 13 communities: Avondale, Buckeye, El Mirage, Glendale, Goodyear, Litchfield Park, Peoria, Sun City, Sun City West, Surprise, Tolleson, Wickenburg, and Youngtown. It's considered one of the fastest-growing regions in Arizona.

GLENDALE

The largest of the West Valley cities is Glendale. It began in 1892 as a religious settlement, but its proximity to Phoenix and the Santa Fe Railroad inspired opportunity and growth. During World War II, Glendale became home to Luke Air Force Base, today the largest training base for the U.S. Air Force; over the latter half of the 20th century, the city grew to more than 200,000 people. Today as the home of two professional sports teams—the Arizona Cardinals (NFL) and Phoenix Coyotes (NHL)—host to the NCAA's Fiesta Bowl, and home to 8 spring training teams Glendale is quickly becoming a sports lovers' paradise. The downtown historic districts attract more than a million visitors a year.

Despite all the changes, Glendale's heritage remains a big part of its charm. Visitors and residents can enjoy a

University of Phoenix Stadium in Glendale

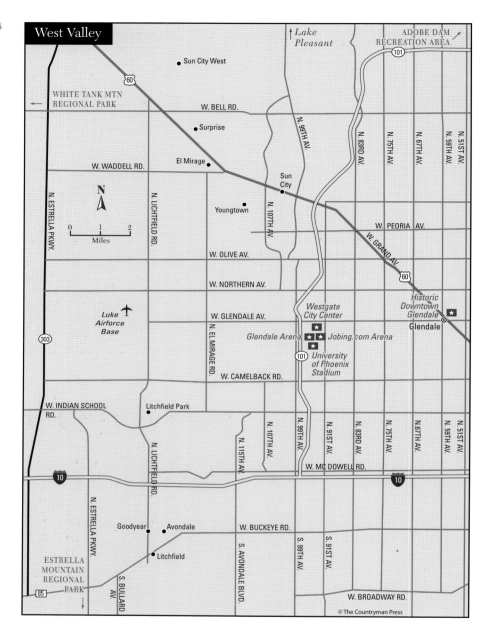

West Valley

Lake Pleasant

ADOBE DAM RECREATION AREA

Sun City West

WHITE TANK MTN REGIONAL PARK

W. BELL RD.

Surprise

El Mirage

W. WADDELL RD.

Sun City

Youngtown

W. PEORIA AV.

W. GRAND AV.

W. OLIVE AV.

W. NORTHERN AV.

Historic Downtown Glendale

Glendale

Luke Airforce Base

W. GLENDALE AV.

Westgate City Center

Glendale Arena   Jobing.com Arena

University of Phoenix Stadium

W. CAMELBACK RD.

W. INDIAN SCHOOL RD.

Litchfield Park

W. MC DOWELL RD.

Goodyear   Avondale

W. BUCKEYE RD.

Litchfield

ESTRELLA MOUNTAIN REGIONAL PARK

W. BROADWAY RD.

N. ESTRELLA PKWY.   N. LICHTFIELD RD.   N. 107TH AV.   N. 99TH AV.   N. 83RD AV.   N. 75TH AV.   N. 67TH AV.   N. 59TH AV.   N. 51ST AV.   N. EL MIRAGE RD.   N. 115TH AV.   N. 91ST AV.   S. AVONDALE BLVD.   S. 99TH AV.   S. 91ST AV.   S. BULLARD AV.

N
0 1 2
Miles

© The Countryman Press

Did you know? Glendale hosted Super Bowl XLII in 2008 and is also home to *American Idol* winner Jordin Sparks and Grammy winner Marty Robbins, of "El Paso" fame.

weekly art walk through the historic downtown, visit sites like the Sahuaro and Manistee ranches, browse the city's 90 antique and specialty shops, and tour the Cerreta Candy Company, a family-owned chocolate factory that

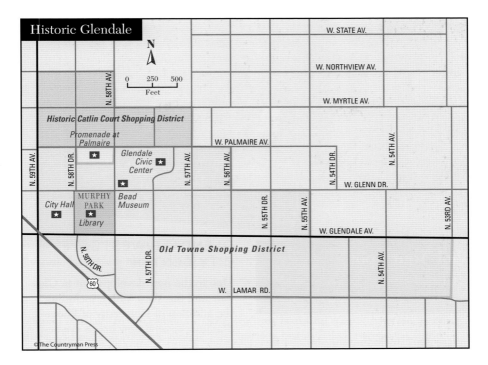

Historic Glendale

N

0   250   500
Feet

Historic Catlin Court Shopping District

Promenade at Palmaire

W. STATE AV.

W. NORTHVIEW AV.

W. MYRTLE AV.

W. PALMAIRE AV.

Glendale Civic Center

City Hall   MURPHY PARK   Bead Museum

Library

Old Towne Shopping District

W. GLENN DR.

W. GLENDALE AV.

W. LAMAR RD.

N. 59TH AV.   N. 58TH DR.   N. 58TH AV.   N. 57TH AV.   N. 56TH AV.   N. 55TH DR.   N. 55TH AV.   N. 54TH DR.   N. 54TH AV.   N. 53RD AV.   N. 57TH DR.   N. 58TH DR.

© The Countryman Press

Luke Air Force Base (www.luke.af.mil), which, like many of the area's airports, opened during World War II, remains an active air force base and has trained almost 50,000 pilots since that time. It is considered the largest fighter training base in the Western world, with more than 180 aircraft, 7,000 military and reserve members, and 1,500 civilian employees. Base tours are available for organized groups between 15 and 40 people Monday–Friday 8–4. Restrictions and conditions apply; call 623-856-5853 for more information or to schedule a tour.

About 200,000 guests a year enjoy **Luke Days Air Show,** which typically takes place in late March. This two-day show includes aerial demonstrations by the Thunderbirds, the U.S. Air Force's Aerial Demonstration Team; ground displays, including vintage aircraft; and attractions and exhibits. General admission is free, although a $5 parking fee may apply in certain areas.

has been around since the late 1970s. Country music and NASCAR fans might enjoy a visit in the hometown of country music legend Marty Robbins. But while the past may be the foundation of Glendale's charm, the city has fast-forwarded into the 21st century with the recent addition of University of Phoenix Stadium—the most state-of-the-art football venue in the country—and Westgate City Center, a futuristic shopping experience straight out of *Back to the Future Part II*.

in 2006, serves good Mexican American fare at affordable prices. Join them Friday and Sunday for live entertainment, and on the second Saturday of each month for Comedy Club. Die-hard breakfast fans have been known to traverse the Valley for Bit-zee's large and delicious breakfast menu.

If you like this . . . check out Glendale's Downtown Dining District (www.visitglendale.com/downtown diningdistrict) for more great indie restaurants.

Haus Murphy's (623-939-2480; www.hausmurphys.com) is the perfect place for lovers of German fare; here they will find a restaurant after their own hearts. The schnitzel, sausage, sauerbraten, and German beers have Valley visitors coming back year after year. The beer garden offers a wonderful outdoor dining experience. Enjoy live entertainment Friday–Sunday nights. And don't forget to try the apple strudel.

Also in the historic district is ZANG Asian Bistro (623-847-8888; www.zangasianbistro.com), featuring Asian-influenced dishes inspired by the travels of owner David Chang and global experiences of Executive Chef Kim Ming Poon. This restaurant features fine dining for a pleasant price. Dishes reflect the cuisines of China, Japan, Indonesia, Malaysia, Singapore, and Vietnam.

Westgate City Center (near the University of Phoenix Stadium, where the Arizona Cardinals play football, and Jobing.com Arena, where the Phoenix Coyotes play hockey) offers another concentrated dining district in the West Valley.

Glendale

Thee Pitts Again (602-996-7488; www.theepittsagain.com) is a 1950s-style restaurant that specializes in barbecued meats and strange fried delicacies like fried pickles or rattlesnake, along with pulled pork and beef brisket. You can even get a fried Twinkie.

Cucina Tagliani Italian Kitchen (602-547-2782; www.cucinatagliani.com), a family-owned restaurant, has been heralded locally as one of "the best Italian restaurants in the Valley." Tasty, traditional Italian dishes and enormous portions (even the half-sized pasta bowls are fit for two) make this a Valley favorite, and their dessert menu puts them over the top. The chocolate mascarpone cake is absolutely decadent and sized to serve at least three, so bring friends.

If you like this . . . try one of their other two locations in Peoria and Avondale.

Peoria

In Peoria, Dillon's (623-979-5353; www.dillonsrestaurant.com) specializes in barbecued and smoked meats and serves a homestyle menu complete with homemade cobbler and award-winning onion rings. Locals love the food and the atmosphere.

Litchfield/Goodyear

For authentic Mexican, head to Arturo's Mexican Food Restaurant and Lounge (623-932-0241; 13290 W. Van Buren, Goodyear). Family owned and operated, Arturo's has served the West Valley Sonoran-style fare for 50 years.

Located at the historic Wigwam Resort (they celebrated 80 years in 2009), Arizona Kitchen (623-935-3811; www.wigwamresort.com) is an award-winning restaurant serving Sonoran-inspired dishes. The incredibly flavorful menu includes entrées like king salmon, Kobe short ribs, and chile-rubbed maple leaf duck. Staff are attentive, and the setting is uniquely Southwest, with an old adobe fireplace and Native American pottery.

BAR AND GRILLS

McDuffy's Peoria (623-334-5000; www.mcduffys.com/peoria), originally located off Tempe's Mill Avenue, moved to Peoria several years ago. Off-track betting, 90-plus televisions and jumbo screens, and close proximity to the Peoria Sports Complex make this a favorite of sports lovers. Full menu of standard American food; check out their lunch specials. There's a second location in the East Valley, in Chandler (480-966-8200).

CAFÉS

A Touch of European Café (623-847-7119; 7146 N. 57th Drive), located in the historic Caitlin Court District of downtown Glendale, has been discovered by *The New Yorker.* Husband-and-wife team Waldemor and Malgorzata Okula, originally from Poland, own and operate this little café (just five tables!) out of a tiny cottage. Try the borscht, hunter's stew, and pierogi. Call first; hours are limited.

FAST FOOD

Pete's Fish & Chips (623-937-6001; www.petesfishandchips.com), a local favorite in downtown Glendale since 1947, serves fried fish, shrimp, oysters, scallops, burgers, and dogs. It's all tasty without being too greasy, portions are nicely sized, and prices are good. Pete's has been a local favorite for more than 60 years, so they must be doing some-

ANTIQUING IN GLENDALE
Located within Historic Old Town Glendale are a number of well-known (at least locally) antique shops, including **A Mad Hatter's Antiques** (623-931-1991; www.amadhatter.com). The store boasts more than 20,000 square feet of both new and antique items, including vintage clothing, books, art glass and pottery, Western décor, china, and a year-round display of Christmas ornaments. **The Apple Tree** (623-435-8486; www.picture trail.com), considered one of the area's oldest shops, offers antique home décor and reproductions of antique pieces. You can also check out **Bo's Funky Stuff** (623-842-0220; 5605 West Glendale Avenue) for unique antique finds you'd be hard pressed to find elsewhere. Also on Glendale Avenue are **Empire Antiques** (623-931-0558) and **Antique Haven** (623-939-3420).

thing right! Well-kept property and friendly staff; drive through or sit on the patio. There are seven additional locations Valley-wide, including Phoenix, Tempe, and Mesa.

48 Hours

If you don't have much time to spend here, or if you've only allocated a couple of days of your vacation to the West Valley, this short-trip itinerary will give you an idea of what to do while you're here. While two days is not enough time to do everything here, it's plenty of time catch some of the best of what the area offers.

Quick tip: Did you know . . . one of Glendale's claims to fame is as the birthplaceof country music legend and two-time Grammy Award winner Marty Robbins. Robbins won a Grammy each for his 1959 hit "El Paso" and 1970 hit "My Woman, My Woman, My Wife". Robbins was born in Glendale in 1925 and died in 1982, the same year he was elected to the Country Music Hall of Fame.

Westgate City Center

GETTING THERE

If you're staying at the Renaissance Glendale Hotel & Spa, you're a short walk away; however, if you're staying at one of the other West Valley hotels, Westgate City Center (www.westgate citycenter.com) is south of Glendale Avenue between the Loop 101 West and 91st Avenue. Conveniently located adjacent to University of Phoenix Cardinal Stadium and Jobing.com Arena, this colorful, futuristic outdoor shopping and dining hot spot features stories-high billboards, water and light shows, and an urban mix of retail, office, and living space.

If you're looking to stop for drinks and appetizers, enjoy the half-off drinks and appetizers happy hour at Saddle Ranch Chop House (623-889-7770; www.srrestaurants.com), at the south end of Westgate City Center, or salmon sashimi and hot sake at Kabuki (623-772-9832; www.kabuki restaurants.com).

In the mood for something a little more substantial? For a Western dining

Outdoor shopping at Westgate City Center

Saddle Ranch Chop House

experience, head to Saddle Ranch Chop House, where you'll find cowboy food—steaks and burgers—as well as salads, wraps, and seafood. You can also ride the mechanical bull and stay for late-night entertainment and eats (they have a special menu 1:45–3:30 AM daily). For a laid-back Jimmy Buffet–style dinner, put your feet up, order a margarita, and chill at Jimmy Buffet's Margaritaville (623-772-0011; www.margaritavilleglendale.com).

If you like this . . . try their Old Town Scottsdale location. The original Saddle Ranch Chop House opened on the Sunset Strip in 1999.

You have a couple of options for after-dinner entertainment, from the raucous dueling piano bar The Shout! House (623-772-1500; www.theshout house.com/Glendale/home.asp) to a live concert at the adjacent Jobing.com Arena (623-773-3200; www. jobing arena.com), home of the Phoenix Coyotes and host to performances by entertainers such as Elton John,

Jimmy Buffet's Margaritaville

Quick tip: Be sure to pick your show and order tickets in advance, either online via the Jobing.com Arena Web site or through Ticketmaster (800-745-3000; www.ticketmaster.com).

Christina Aguilera, and the Harlem Globetrotters. Or settle for a quiet Arizona evening beneath the stars watching Glendale's version of the Bellagio's dancing fountains at Waterdance Plaza. A series of fountains synchronized to music and video components put on their display every half hour beginning at 10 AM.

DAY 1

Breakfast

You'll need a hearty breakfast before your hike; breakfast at Bit-zee Mama's (623-931-0562; www.historic-glendale.net/bitzee_mama's.htm)—a blend of Mexican and American comfort foods in an old-style vinyl and Formica-covered tables kind of restaurant—will make you feel like a Glendale native. Or chow down like a cowboy posthike at the Saddle Ranch Chop House (623-889-7770; www.srrestaurants.com), where they serve brunch daily 11–3. They serve the works: pancakes, Texas toast, huevos rancheros, sausage 'n' biscuits, hash browns, and bacon.

Take a Hike

The Petroglyph Trail at the Deer Valley Rock Art Center (623-582-8007; www.asu.edu/clas/shesc/dvrac) in north Phoenix (north of the Loop 101 and west of I-17) features one of the best displays of Native American rock art in

the Valley. Along this handicapped-accessible 0.25-mile trail, you'll find plenty of desert flora and fauna. The trail leads to a jumble of boulders covered with ancient symbols carved by some of Arizona's first inhabitants.

If a 0.25-mile walk isn't enough, work up a sweat among the more than 15 miles of paths that comprise the trail system at Thunderbird Conservation Park (623-930-2820; www.glendaleaz.com/ParksandRecreation/parksandfacilities/thunderbirdpark.cfm) in Glendale (just north of the Loop 101 on 59th Avenue). As it's open sunrise to sunset, you can get an early start hiking among the Hedgepeth Hills

Quick tip: Be wary of the directions you find online; instead visit the Rock Art Center's Web site (http://dvrac.asu.edu/visit/hours-directions) for how to get here from anywhere in the Valley.

Did you know . . . that the name *Thunderbird* (so prevalent in the West Valley) is inspired by the World War II fighter pilot training facility established in Glendale in 1939? The airfield itself was designed to resemble the mythical "super" bird of Native American cultures. The bird is said to embody power and strength for many, including the Anasazi in Arizona. During World War II, thousands of pilots trained at Thunderbird Field until it closed in 1945.

Today, Thunderbird Field #1 (thus named after Thunderbird Field #2 opened in Scottsdale in 1941) is the site of the Thunderbird School of Global Management, established in 1946 by Lt. Gen. Barton Kyle Yount, commanding general of the U.S. Army Air Training Command.

There are charming shops in Historic Downtown Glendale

(named for early homesteader Robert Hedgepeth). On your hike, you'll find the saguaro cactus—majestic sentinel of the Sonoran Desert—as well as its prickly brethren and a multitude of desert plants and animals.

Stop for Lunch

If breakfast wasn't enough to tide you over, stop for lunch in Glendale at Haus Murphy's (623-939-2480; www.hausmurphys.com) and load up on the carbs for an afternoon of sightseeing—they have all of the favorites: gnocchi, schnitzel, potato pancakes. No worries, in addition to all of their bratwursts, sausages, and grilled Reubens, you'll also find a couple of gourmet salads filled with lighter fare.

You can also enjoy a cold brew in their biergarten.

Afternoon Sight-Seeing

Walk off lunch with a trip through Historic Downtown Glendale (www .historic-glendale.net). The area hosts many annual festivals, from the delicious Glendale Chocolate Affaire in February to the delightful Glendale Jazz and Blues Festival in April. Historic Downtown Glendale covers 10 square blocks near the intersection of US 60 (Grand Avenue) and 59th and Glendale avenues. Three separate districts comprise the area: Caitlin Court, a series of converted bungalows along tree-lined avenues; the gaslight district of Old Towne, in the blocks around Murphy Park; and the new Promenade at Palmaire, home of the Glendale Visitor Center, shops, and restaurants, and a six-hundred-space parking garage. Each of the districts features unique shops, boutiques, restaurants, cafés, and coffeehouses. Also in this area is The Bead Museum (623-931-2737; www.beadmuseumaz.org) and its 100,000 beads and beaded artifacts, and Glendale's own Cerreta Candy Company (623-930-1000; www.cerreta .com), which offers 30-minute and self-guided tours of its chocolate factory.

Quick tip: If there's an event, keep in mind that parking may be difficult, but not impossible—there are about two thousand parking spots within a 10-minute walk of the downtown district. To be prepared, check the event Web site, www .glendaleaz.com/events, for parking and event maps. The city often provides free parking at Glendale Community College and a free shuttle service to and from the event.

Murphy Park

Dinner

For dinner, get dressed up (in Arizona this means a nice pair of shorts) and head to the historic Wigwam Golf Resort & Spa to the award-winning Red's Steakhouse (623-935-3811; www.redssteakhouse.com) for a delicious culinary treat created by Chef de Cuisine Michael Scott. Expect to pay first-class prices for this world-class meal. Arrive early for Red Hot Happy Hour at The Bar at Red's; order your drink and relax beside the outdoor fireplace while you wait to be seated. Scott incorporates local flavors and puts a contemporary twist on his menu of steak and seafood. Stay late and enjoy the live, local entertainment.

The restaurant honors V. O. "Red" Allen, the first golf professional (and the first of three generations of Allen family golfers) to serve the Wigwam. Today, Red's grandson, Craig Allen, is the Wigwam's Director of Golf, a position he has held since 2001.

DAY 2

Breakfast

Get a final taste of Arizona's incredible weather with breakfast at Verrado Grille (623-388-3013; www.ravenat verrado.com) at the Raven Golf Course in Buckeye, just east of the White Tank Mountains. Breakfast includes treats like banana walnut pancakes, biscuits and gravy, and the breakfast quesadilla. The golf course setting and patio seating options make this restaurant a relaxing morning. (It's also a great afternoon choice—and breathtaking at sunset.)

Shopping

Drink in the blue skies before you head home, and explore the shops at Westgate City Center (www.west gateaz.com), located adjacent to University of Phoenix Cardinal

Stadium and Glendale Arena (Jobing .com Arena). This colorful, futuristic plaza features a number of shoe, sports, apparel, accessory and speciality stores and almost twenty restaurants and bars.

Lunch Before You Go
Have lunch at the trendy Tuscan Oven (623-877-4760; www.biceglendale .com), a little Italian bistro at Westgate City Center. Enjoy pasta, paninis, pizzas, gourmet salads, soups, and entrées with combinations that pique the senses: pine nuts and pesto, veal and spinach, or prosciutto and fresh mozzarella.

Extend Your Stay

If you have more time, try these great places to see and things to do . . .

ARIZONA HERITAGE

Peoria Arizona Historical Society (623-487-8030; 10304 N. 83rd Avenue, Peoria) museum—converted from a two-room school—preserves and shares the history of the area. Its exhibits include antique dolls, a doctor's buggy, old quilts, and a 1900 kitchen corner. Wander the blacksmith shop, dairy, and other exhibits as part of the agricultural museum while you await your scheduled tour of the 1939 jail— original cells and all.

Sahuaro Ranch (623-930-2820; www.glendaleaz.com/srpha) was once the home of William Henry Bartlett, who originally homesteaded Sahuaro Ranch in 1886. By 1891 he controlled more than 2,000 acres and was considered one of the largest ranchers in the area. In its heyday Sahuaro Ranch was a beautiful, parklike estate with rosebushes, palm trees, and a pond with a bridge leading to an island gazebo. At one time or another alfalfa, fig trees, citrus trees, and cotton had been planted on the original 640-acre farm. In 1927 Richard W. Smith purchased the ranch and planted citrus, pecan, and date groves. When Smith died in 1944, he left the ranch to his son Richard S. Smith, and in 1966 the city of Glendale began the 11-year process of purchasing 80 of those original 640 acres. Today the city's holdings include 17 acres that have been placed on the National Register of Historic Places, including the ranch's first permanent dwelling—the Adobe House, built in 1887, as well as the original fruit-packing shed, foreman's house, barnyard, and guest house, all built in the latter part of the 19th century. The ranch is located next to Glendale Community College and provides a softball field, volleyball courts, soccer fields, and a dog park to the surrounding community. For historical tours, call 623-930-4200.

A part of Arizona State University's College of Liberal Arts and Sciences, Deer Valley Rock Art Center (623-582-8007; www.asu.edu/clas/shesc /dvrac) in north Phoenix is protector of the Valley's largest concentration of Native American rock art. It features an interpretive trail that will take you among hundreds of ancient drawings called petroglyphs; the 47-acre facility encompasses a museum, archaeological site, nature preserve, and research center. The museum provides historical information about the drawings and the area. The trail closes half an hour before the museum. Guided tours available parts of the year; call for availability.

That Thursday Thing (623-930-4500; www.visitglendale.com), in Glendale, is an excellent opportunity to tour Historic Downtown Glendale on the third Thursday of the month and enjoy live entertainment, free horse-drawn carriage rides, art, and more. There is usually a theme and free trolley service. Area shops extend their hours, and live entertainment peppers the sidewalks.

Located 1 block north of Glendale Avenue at 58th Avenue (next to the Glendale Civic Center) in Historic Downtown Glendale, The Bead Museum (623-931-2737; www.beadmuseum az.org) is home to an international collection of more than 100,000 beads and beaded artifacts. These are not your average beads—many items are handmade, ceremonial artifacts and representative of talent and cultural traditions from all over the world. Guided tours, group tours, and workshops are available; call the museum educator to schedule tours and workshops in advance.

For more than 25 years, the West Valley Art Museum (623-972-0635; www.wvam.org) in Surprise has focused primarily on the visual works of Arizona artists and collections from cultures around the world, particularly in Asian, Latin American, and African regions. The museum's permanent collection represents four thousand pieces, a quarter of them including ethnic dress, materials, and artifacts such as Japanese woodcut prints and Chinese snuff bottles. The collection includes three hundred prints from artists such as Andy Warhol and T. C. Cannon and works by well-known Arizona artists, including Ann Coe and John Waddell.

The four-hundred-seat Arizona Broadway Theatre (623-776-8400;

www.azbroadwaytheatre.com), off Bell Road and the Loop 101, next to the Peoria Sports Complex, is the northwest Valley's answer to professional theater. Regaling patrons with classical Broadway musicals and an elegant dinner menu, Arizona Broadway Theatre is a popular and entertaining venue.

Other area museums include the Smithsonian-affiliated Challenger Space Center (623-322-2001; www.az challenger.org), which features, among other exhibits, the Columbia Shuttle Memorial Display, in honor of the crew members who perished February 1, 2003; a meteorite exhibit on loan from ASU's Center for Meteorite Study; and a display depicting the history of the space program. While the museum focuses on educational programming, they also offer a variety of opportunities for the general public, including a simulated space mission, planetarium shows, and telescope classes and stargazing events for families at various times throughout the year. The center is a large white building located on 83rd Avenue in Peoria, adjacent to Sunrise Mountain High School and accessible from the Loop 101.

OUTDOOR ADVENTURES

As with all of Arizona, the West Valley is a rich repository of outdoor adventures—from hiking in the Estrella Mountains to boating on Lake Pleasant, there is plenty to do.

Parks

Located south of I-10 close to Phoenix International Raceway, Estrella Mountain Regional Park (623-932-3911; www.maricopa.gov/parks/estrella) covers almost 20,000 acres and provides space for camping, hiking, biking, running, horseback riding, fishing, golfing, and picnicking. Campsites are the developed kind, which means you'll find water and electrical hookups along with the typical picnic table and fire ring. The park features more than 30 trails that can accommodate hikers, mountain bikers, and horseback riders, as well as a series of competitive tracks totaling 13 miles. The tracks are usually used by mountain bikers; however, horseback riders and runners have been known to use the trails for training purposes. The park recommends the technical loop (2.86 miles) for experts only. The park's Web site provides an excellent set of trail maps that you can print.

Located at the confluence of the Gila and Agua Fria rivers, the park features catch-and-release fishing along the banks of the Gila River. Renovated in 1998, the Estrella Mountain Golf Course (623-932-3714; www.estrella -golf.com) features a traditional parkland-style par 71 course for golfers of all levels.

Lake Pleasant Regional Park (928-501-1710; www.maricopa.gov /parks/lake_pleasant), located in the northwest Valley, approximately 15 miles north of Sun City, provides developed campsites with electrical and water hookups, dump station, restrooms, picnic tables, and grills. In addition to camping, the park offers boating, fishing, swimming, and hiking trails. Call for more information and to obtain permits. Lake Pleasant is a popular site during the hotter months and an excellent escape from urban life during the cooler part of the year.

Lake Pleasant provides the only shoreline camping experience (for $5) of the county parks. Boaters can enter this expansive body of water from one of two launching ramps. Both have restroom facilities and paved parking lots; they're functional to a water elevation of 1,600 feet.

At 30,000 acres, White Tank Mountain Regional Park (623-935-2505; www.maricopa.gov/parks/white _tank) is Maricopa County's largest regional park. It provides the mountainous backdrop on the Valley's west side. It features 25 miles of multiuse trails as well as a 10-mile competitive track designed for fast-paced mountain bikers, runners, and horseback riders at a trot/gallop. White Tank's 40 campsites are considered semiprimitive; there are no electrical or water hookups, but grills, picnic tables, and comfort stations with showers are available. Note that Olive Avenue becomes White Tank Mountain Road, where the park is located.

White Tanks Riding Stables (623-935-7455; www.whitetanksriding.com) offers guided riding tours November– April. One-hour rides start at about $40 per person, and children seven and under can ride a pony for 20 minutes (about $20 per child). Wagon rides are available. The stables are located at 20300 W. Olive Avenue in Waddell and open November through April.

If you like this . . . try the Cave Creek Trail Rides at Cave Creek Regional Park or Ponderosa Stables (602-268-1261; www.arizona-horses .com) at South Mountain Park in Phoenix.

Once part of the Maricopa County Regional Parks System, Thunderbird Conservation Park (623-930-2820; www.glendaleaz.com/ParksandRecre ation/parksandfacilities/thunderbird park.cfm) is now owned and operated by the city of Glendale. This 1,100-plus-acre park features 20 miles of trails; activities include hiking, mountain biking, running, horseback riding, picnicking, and four viewing blinds—the better to catch a glimpse of desert fauna. Three of these blinds are accessible

The Home of the Arizona Cardinals

University of Phoenix Stadium in Glendale, Arizona—home of the Arizona Cardinals—opened in August 2006. This amazing feat of technology and horticulture was designed by internationally known architect Peter Eisenman in conjunction with HOK Sport, Hunt Construction Group, and Urban Earth Design. Intended to capture its desert home, the stadium's exterior skin represents a barrel cactus, while the alternating panels of metal reflect the ever-changing desert light.

Its 18.9-million-pound retractable field tray makes natural grass play possible, even in the desert. But this isn't the only thing that makes the new stadium the NFL's "most technologically advanced." Try the 650 high-definition televisions, two high-resolution video scoreboards, 88 luxury lofts, three party suites,

University of Phoenix Stadium in Glendale

7,500 club seats, two 39,000-square-foot VIP Club Lounges, full air-conditioning, two *huge* noise "thermometers" that gauge how loud the crowd is, and, amazingly, a retractable translucent roof that brings the outdoors in without the full blast of the Phoenix sun. On top of it all, this $455 million stadium is protected by 1/16th inch of "Bird-Air" fabric strong enough to withstand 11,000 pounds per square foot!

In addition to hosting crazy Cardinals fans, it has also welcomed Super Bowl XLII in 2008, the Monster Truck Rally, Tostitos Fiesta Bowl in 2007, and the BCS National Championship Game in 2007, among many other events, concerts, and trade shows.

Tours are available Thursday–Saturday depending on event schedules. To tour this state-of-the-art facility, purchase tickets via Ticketmaster (480-784-4444; www.ticketmaster.com/venue/246628) or at the University of Phoenix Stadium box office (602-379-0102). Tours run about one and a quarter hours and require about a mile of walking, so wear comfortable shoes. Tours are wheelchair accessible. Note that it's best to order your tickets in advance since tours can sell out.

Stadium in Glendale—typically falls in late December or early January.

In the last decade and a half, the West Valley has created a haven for spring training Cactus League teams and their fans. In 2009 alone, the West Valley introduced two new stadiums: Camelback Ranch—Glendale and

Goodyear Ballpark in Goodyear; during the 2009 and 2010 spring training seasons combined, a total of four new teams entered the Phoenix-area fold.

The Peoria Sports Complex (623-773-8720; www.peoriaaz.gov/spring training), built in 1994, hosts both the San Diego Padres (www.padres.com)

Jobing.com Arena

and Seattle Mariners (www.mariners.org) on 145 acres of land and features a stadium for more than 11,000 cheering fans. Surprise Stadium (623-222-2222; www.surprisespringtraining.com) was built in 2002 to host the Kansas City Royals (www.kcroyals.com) and Texas Rangers (http://texas.rangers.mlb.com).

In 2009, the City of Glendale added Camelback Ranch—Glendale (623-302-5000; www.camelbackranch baseball.com), the new spring training home of the Los Angeles Dodgers (http://losangeles.dodgers.mlb.com) and the Chicago White Sox (http://chicago.whitesox.mlb.com), to the Cactus League roster. The recently completed Camelback Ranch complex, in addition to baseball fields and 118,000 square feet of clubhouse space

(major and minor), features 141 acres with walking paths, desert landscaping, a 1,300-square-foot lake, and the league's largest spring training stadium. Also completed in time for the 2009 spring training season, Goodyear Ballpark (623-882-3130; www.goodyear az.gov), which seats about 10,000 fans, welcomed the Cleveland Indians (http://cleveland.indians.mlb.com) in 2009. The Indians were joined by fellow Ohio team the Cincinnati Reds (http://cincinnati.reds.mlb.com) for the 2010 season.

For more information, visit www.cactus-league.com or each team's individual site; tickets start around $5 and are available online, on-site, or by phone. Please note that most stadiums do not allow food and beverage, large bags, or coolers.

5

Sedona
THE RED ROCK VORTEX

About 115 miles north of Phoenix along I-17—tucked among towering monoliths, sandwiched between the Prescott and Coconino national forests, and straddling the lush greenery of Oak Creek—is Sedona. Named after the wife of T. C. Schnebly, in collaboration with the U.S. Postal Service, the city has become synonymous with the rich hues and breathtaking scenery of red rock country. Like the rest of the state, Sedona is a unique combination of mountainous terrain, beautiful weather, and incredible scenery. But the vibrant contrast of fire red rocks, lush green vegetation, and sapphire blue skies make for an awe-inspiring experience unlike anything you've ever seen. Take one look, and you'll stop wondering why *USA Weekend* named Sedona the most beautiful place in the United States.

Many who visit, however, wonder if there's even more than mere beauty. Simultaneously a place of activity and calm, Sedona seems to infuse visitors with a peaceful tranquillity. Amid all the strolling tourists and bustle of activity, you can find pockets of quietude; moments to pause, look up at the surrounding buttes and mesas, and know that you are somewhere special. Explanations abound as to what makes Sedona unique—the metaphysical power of its vortexes, the intense electromagnetic energy given off by all that oxidized iron (the red in the rocks), or simply the clean air and beautiful views. Wherever the power originates, visitors seem to agree that Sedona is an uplifting experience.

Sedona is a mere two-hour, 113-mile drive from the Valley of the Sun. For the

> **Quick tip:** For a more scenic route and to visit the old mining town of Jerome along the way, turn off I-17 at exit 262; take AZ 69 west (toward Cordes Junction Road /Prescott) all the way to Fain Road. Turn right onto Fain and continue to AZ 89A. The road is winding with steep sides as you climb through the Prescott National Forest. You'll leave behind the plains and ascend into ponderosa pines. (See the "Side Trips" chapter for more about Jerome.)

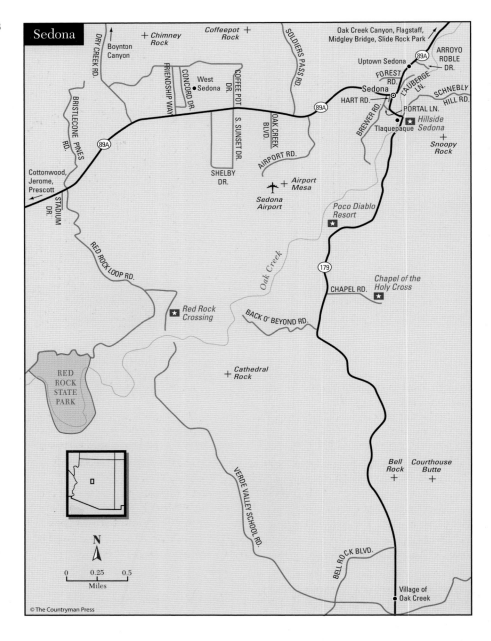

Sedona

Boynton Canyon

Chimney Rock

Coffeepot Rock

Soldiers Pass Rd.

Oak Creek Canyon, Flagstaff, Midgley Bridge, Slide Rock Park

Uptown Sedona

ARROYO ROBLE DR.

FOREST RD.

L'AUBERGE LN.

SCHNEBLY HILL RD.

Sedona

HART RD.

Dry Creek Rd.

Friendship Way

Concord Dr.

Coffee Pot Dr.

West Sedona

S. Sunset Dr.

Oak Creek Blvd.

Airport Rd.

Bristlecone Pines Rd.

Cottonwood, Jerome, Prescott

Stadium Dr.

Shelby Dr.

Sedona Airport

Airport Mesa

Brewer Rd.

Portal Ln.

Tlaquepaque

Hillside Sedona

Snoopy Rock

Poco Diablo Resort

Red Rock Loop Rd.

Oak Creek

Chapel Rd.

Chapel of the Holy Cross

Red Rock Crossing

Back O' Beyond Rd.

Cathedral Rock

RED ROCK STATE PARK

Verde Valley School Rd.

Bell Rock

Courthouse Butte

N

0   0.25   0.5
Miles

Bell Rock Blvd.

Village of Oak Creek

© The Countryman Press

most straightforward route, take I-17 north to exit 298. Pick up AZ 179 and continue for about 14 miles, then turn right onto AZ 89A into Sedona.

Two main highways run through red rock country. AZ 179 diverges from I-17 and heads in a more or less north–south direction from I-17 through the Village of Oak Creek, then past Bell Rock, where it winds its way to the second highway, AZ 89A. AZ 89A bisects Sedona on an east–west course from Cottonwood/Clarkdale

Red Rock vistas

through West Sedona and Uptown, where it heads north through Slide Rock National Park to Flagstaff.

Sedona itself can be divided into three main regions: the Village of Oak Creek, south of town on 179; Uptown Sedona, the Main Street shopping area along 89A headed north of the Y; and West Sedona, on 89A south of the Y, where you'll find the library, the hospital, grocery shopping, and the Sedona–Oak Creek Airport. "The Y" is what locals call the juncture of AZ 179 and AZ 89A.

Sedona RoadRunner (928-282-0938; www.roadrunner.az.gov), a free shuttle, circulates among Sedona's most popular locations, including Hillside Sedona, Tlaquepaque Arts & Crafts Village, and Uptown Sedona. The shuttle runs daily 10–6 and stops about every 10 minutes at designated locations along its 1.3-mile route. (The shuttle doesn't run Thanksgiving, Christmas, and New Year's.)

Pick Your Spot

Best places to stay in Sedona, and what you'll find nearby . . .

Sedona offers the weary traveler everything from cabins to bed & breakfasts to upscale resorts. Depending upon how you want to experience the area, you might be interested in some of the top choices available.

There are number of hotel and resort options available in Sedona and the Village of Oak Creek, ranging from no-frills establishments to luxury resorts complete with golf course and spa. Prices range from less than $100 to $2,000 a night and depend upon the time of year. Most rooms seem to hover around $200–350.

Staying in the Village of Oak Creek puts you on the south end of the Sedona area and close to Bell Rock vortex, Northern Bell, and Courthouse Butte, as well as the iconic Chapel of the Holy Cross, off Chapel Road on the east side of AZ 179. To the west of AZ 179, you'll find Castle Rock, the Cathedral Rock vortex, and the Crescent Moon Recreation Center. There are a number of trailheads to pick up in this area, as well as shopping centers, golf courses, and an outlet center.

Oak Creek, Sedona   Photo courtesy Jacqueline Kinsella

Lodging options include the Hilton Sedona Resort & Spa (928-284-4040 or 877-2-REDROCK; www .hiltonsedona.com), a 219-suite resort on the Sedona Resort Golf Course, featuring an on-site restaurant and bar, three pools, children's programs, and a fitness center. Room amenities include fireplace, wet bar with microwave, and private balcony or patio. Hilton Sedona Resort & Spa has both a championship golf course and a full-service spa offering body wraps, massages, and facials; for more information, visit www.hilton sedonaspa.com.

Equidistant between the Village of Oak Creek and the attractions of Tlaquepaque Arts & Crafts Village, Hillside Sedona, and Uptown Sedona is the Poco Diablo Resort (928-282-7333 or 877-282-5755; www.pocodiablo .com). Located in a residential neighborhood just off AZ 179, the resort features 22 acres, patio and garden rooms, massage therapy, a nine-hole golf course, and a heated pool and spa.

Did you know? Chapel of the Holy Cross, shown on this book's cover, was designed by sculptress Marguerite Brunswig Staude. Staude, a devout Catholic, who envisioned a version of the church in 1932 after she first saw the Empire State Building. After she spent years of reworking the design and choosing the right site, the construction crew broke ground in 1955, and the finished chapel was dedicated in 1957.

SEDONA

Farther north on AZ 179 is Los Abrigados Resort & Spa (928-282-1777 or 800-521-3131; www.ilxresorts.com). Part time-share, part resort property, the 22-acre resort is well placed on the banks of Oak Creek and across the parking lot from Tlaquepaque Village, an arts, crafts, and shopping experience. The property features three award-winning restaurants, two pools, and the Sedona Spa. Additional amenities include on-site miniature golf, pool, and fitness center. Nearby is Hillside Sedona, with a number of art galleries; hiking trails; Camel Head and Snoopy Rock formations; and Uptown Sedona, a short drive away, as is Schnebly Hill Road, just east of 179.

A beautiful winding drive northwest of Sedona brings you to Enchantment Resort (928-282-2900 or 800-826-4180; www.enchantmentresort.com). Located in Boynton Canyon in the Red Rock Secret Wilderness of Coconino National Forest, not far from the Kachina Woman, one of Sedona's four vortexes, the resort is nestled among the tranquillity of Sedona's towering red rock formations. The resort offers swimming, croquet, tennis, hiking, and the Camp Coyote children's program. The resort features six pools, three 18-hole championship golf courses nearby, and three restaurants: Yavapai (fine dining), Tii Gavo (casual dining), and Mii amo Café (healthful dining). The award-winning Mii amo spa (928-203-8500 or 888-749-2137; www.miiamo.com), a 24,000-square-foot facility, offers all-inclusive spa packages and a full menu of treatments and services.

There are more than 20 bed & breakfasts in Sedona and surrounding areas. The Bed & Breakfast Guild of Sedona (800-915-4442; www.bbsedona.net) is an excellent place to find the best one for you. Each offers a unique experience influenced by its particular location and the personality of its owners; you'll find B&Bs that cater to couples, hiking or golf enthusiasts, nature lovers, or those looking to escape the urban rush. They range in size from two-bedroom cottages to 16-room inns.

Enchantment Resort

UPTOWN SEDONA

From 179 take a right onto AZ 89A at the Y, and you'll head into Uptown Sedona, with hundreds of shops, restaurants, art galleries, and attractions. Hotels and resorts include Best Western Arroyo Roble Hotel & Creekside Villas, Amara Hotel, and L'Auberge. There are several trailheads north of Uptown off 89A, the same road that winds its way through Oak Creek Canyon.

The Best Western Arroyo Roble Hotel & Creekside Villas (928-282-4001 or 800-773-3662; www.bestwest ernsedona.com) in Uptown Sedona overlooks Oak Creek Canyon and offers views of the surrounding red rocks. The five-story hotel features king and double-queen rooms with a private patio or balcony to enjoy the amazing views, as well as two-bedroom, 1,300-square-foot creek-side

Towering red rocks at Oak Creek Canyon

Photo courtesy Jacqueline Kinsella

villas, complete with hot tubs, fireplaces, and full kitchens. Hotel amenities include private Oak Creek access, indoor-outdoor heated pools, a fitness room, tennis and racquetball courts, and a steam room/sauna.

A little oasis off the main drag (AZ 89A), Amara Hotel, Restaurant & Spa (928-282-4828 or 866-455-6610; www.amararesort.com) offers the creature comforts of home with a splash of style and an abundance of tranquillity. The hundred-room boutique hotel features lush surroundings overlooking Oak Creek Canyon and dramatic views of the towering red rocks, particularly from the courtyard and outdoor saltwater pool. Only a short walk to the shops, restaurants, galleries, and attractions of Uptown Sedona, the hotel is also home to Hundred Rox restaurant and Serenite Spa. Begin your day with a private yoga lesson or their complimentary breakfast buffet.

L'Auberge de Sedona Resort (928-282-1661 or 800-272-6777; www.lauberge .com), a beautiful European-style resort, features cottages and a lodge; a restaurant that serves French cuisine; and a spa with body wraps, facials, and massages. Try their Signature Seasonal Massage, which incorporates jojoba and essential oils and hydrates and rejuvenates the body (90 minutes, $175). Choose a one- or two-bedroom cottage situated along the creek or in the garden; stay in a guest room or junior suite at the Lodge, with a private patio or balcony; or rent the entire Creek House for a family reunion. Stargaze Friday night with the resort's professional astronomer, or dine at the award-winning restaurant.

If you turn left at the Y, you will head into West Sedona and its many trailheads; in fact, quite a few of the roads off 89A lead to trailheads. Also look for the famous Sphinx, Capitol Butte, Coffee Pot Rock, and Chimney Rock formations. Hotels in this area include Best Western Inn of Sedona, Hampton Inn—Sedona, Kokopelli Suites, and the boutique hotel Sedona Rouge Hotel & Spa.

The award-winning Best Western Inn of Sedona (928-282-3072 or 800-292-6344; www.innofsedona.com) offers incredible views of Sedona's red rocks from its outdoor pool and spa. It features recently upgraded two-bed queen and king rooms, some with a fireplace. Amenities include free Internet access and continental breakfast; vacation packages are available.

A 77-room boutique hotel, Sedona Rouge Hotel & Spa (928-203-4111 or 866-312-4111; www.sedonarouge.com) offers an urban experience with rooms that open onto an open-air courtyard and water fountain. Situated close to some of the area's most iconic red rock features, trailheads, and local restaurants, the hotel features a full-service spa, lush gardens, and an outdoor swimming pool with red rock views. The spa offers massages, facials, body treatments, and spa packages. Amenities include complimentary wireless Internet access and a nightly turndown service. Sedona Rouge is also home to Reds, a bistro-style restaurant serving American favorites infused with flavors from around the world.

Also in West Sedona is the 56-room Hampton Inn—Sedona (928-282-4700; www.hamptoninn.com), featuring an outdoor heated pool and whirlpool, rooms with microwaves and refrigerators, complimentary high-speed Internet access, and a free daily, deluxe continental buffet.

Kokopelli Suites (928-204-1146 [reservations] or 800-789-7393; www.kokopellisuites.com), which opened in 1996, offers large one-room suites with separate sitting areas, a heated pool and spa, and deluxe continental breakfast.

Courtyard at Sedona Rouge

Local Flavors

Taste of the town . . . local restaurants, cafés, bars, bistros, etc.

The demands of Sedona's millions of visitors, many from other countries, have kept local restaurants on their toes. Offering unique, world-class culinary experiences, small-town Sedona has a big-city menu.

RESTAURANTS

Village of Oak Creek
Located at Tequa Festival Marketplace in the Village of Oak Creek, local favorite Cucina Rustica (928-284-3010; www.cucinarustica.com) serves old-world Italian and Mediterranean cuisine. Dine alfresco on the shaded

Uptown Sedona's walking malls boast many shops and eateries

patio, where you can enjoy the cascading waterfall and the panoramic view, or indoors, where the rich rustic decor and friendly service invite you to stay. The food has received rave reviews, and the wine list is extensive, with a healthy selection of wines by the glass.

Sedona
Awarded the Best of Award of Excellence by *Wine Spectator* magazine again in 2009, the Yavapai Restaurant (928-282-2900 or 800-826-4180; www .enchantmentresort.com) at Enchantment Resort features 180-degree views of beautiful Boynton Canyon. Outdoor and indoor seating is available; floor-to-ceiling windows span the dining room, inviting the best of red rock country into your dining experience. Jazz brunch on Sunday (reservations required); no jeans or athletic shoes.

Tlaquepaque Village
Nestled in a quiet corner of Tlaquepaque Arts & Crafts Village, René (928-282-9225; www.rene-sedona.com) has been serving locals and tourists alike since 1977. Designed by Executive Chef Ruben Sandoval, the restaurant's signature dishes incorporate flavors of the Southwest with French, American, and Continental cuisine. Enjoy the award-winning wine list, alfresco dining, and charming ambience.

Uptown Sedona
Dine alfresco beside the open fire pit outside at Amara Hotel's restaurant, Hundred Rox (928-282-4828 or 866-455-6610; www.amararesort.com). The restaurant serves Italian cuisine with a decidedly California influence under the artful hands of Chef David Schmidt (formerly of other well-known Arizona restaurants). His menu includes a blend of organic veggies, pasta, seafood, and beef, with a dash

of the unique—such as the lemon-jalapeño aioli or ale poached Italian sausage. Seating is also available inside beside the floor-to-ceiling windows that overlook the courtyard and lush foliage of nearby Oak Creek.

Cowboy Club Grille and Spirits (928-282-4200; www.cowboyclub.com), also home of the Silver Saddle Room, is housed in a circa-1946 building that was one of only three main buildings in Sedona at the time. Originally the Oak Creek Tavern, it served as combination saloon, pool hall, grocery store, and meeting place. In the mid-1960s—June 23, 1965, to be exact—several cowboy artists sat around the fireplace and organized the well-known Cowboy Artists of America (CAA). Today the Cowboy Club features works by CAA artists, original wooden walls, and some of the best buffalo and Angus steaks around, as well as delicious poultry and seafood. The menu changes seasonally, but you'll find cactus fries and grilled rattlesnake year-round.

If you like this . . . enjoy an upscale dining experience in the rustic elegance of the Silver Saddle Room (no kids' menu here), as well as the same great choices of steak, seafood, and poultry, complete with all the bells and whistles, including appetizer, dessert, and sorbet intermezzo. "Dressy casual" and reservations are recommended for the Silver Saddle Room, where dinner is served 5–10 PM daily.

West Sedona

The Coffee Pot Restaurant (928-282-6626; 2050 W. AZ 89A), a local favorite since the 1950s, has *too* many choices, what with 101 omelets and breakfast served all day; you'll also find Mexican and American dishes and, some say, the best breakfast (and coffee) in Sedona.

Its name may say *café*, but don't let the word throw you. Heartline Café (928-282-0785; www.heartlinecafe .com), owned by Chef Charles Cline and his wife, Phyllis, is definitely an upscale restaurant with an ambience as rich (and delightful) as its food. Inspired by Cline's culinary expertise, the menu is an eclectic mix of Asian, Mediterranean, and European influences, and you'll find both large plates (entrées) and small plates (appetizers) to satisfy your hunger.

BAR AND GRILLS

In Uptown Sedona, at the juncture of Jordan Road and AZ 89A, is Orchards Bar and Grill (928-282-1661 or 877-700-2944; www.orchardsinn.com /dining.php), a charming local favorite that serves traditional American fare—sandwiches, homemade soups, hand-tossed pizzas, pastas, and salads—in a relaxing and inviting atmosphere. You'll also find seafood, steak, and barbecued ribs. Finish off your meal with one of several delectable desserts. Espresso, coffee, and pastries round out a full breakfast menu.

CAFÉS

Village of Oak Creek

Sedona may be a tourist town, but it hasn't wandered too far from its high-desert beginnings. Thus it's no surprise to find a number of café-style eateries serving up hearty, all-American fare. Sprinkled throughout town, along AZ 179 and AZ 89A both north and south of the Y, are choices like the Blue Moon Café (928-284-1831; www.blue mooncafe.us), where they serve break-fast all day, as well as everyday café fare such as burgers, sandwiches, pizza, and homestyle dinners; they serve beer and wine, and boast the best Phillys in town.

Tlaquepaque Village

Secret Garden Café (928-203-9564; www.sedonasecretgardencafe.com) at Tlaquepaque Village serves sandwiches, soups, and salads.

Uptown Sedona

Look for the ever-delicious but definitely decadent Black Cow Café (928-203-9868; 229 N. AZ 89A), where they serve baked goods, coffee, and homemade ice cream daily.

West Sedona

A popular café choice, Chocala Tree (928-282-2997; www.chocolatreecafe.com)—100 percent organic—serves a sugar-free, gluten-free, dairy-free menu with items like sushi, veggie tacos, and Thai noodle salad. Treat your sweet tooth with their delicious handmade chocolates or homemade desserts.

WINE SHOPS

For a taste of Arizona (wine), visit The Art of Wine (877-903-WINE; www.artofwine.com), located in Uptown Sedona at The Shops at Hyatt Piñon Pointe, on the ridge above 89A in Old Town. Try before you buy with their all-day-long wine tastings offered daily. $10 buys you a preview of five wines; $15 buys you a premier tasting of six wines.

48 Hours

If you don't have much time to spend here, or if you've only allocated a couple of days of your vacation to a Sedona visit, this short-trip itinerary will give you an idea of what to do while you're here. While two days is not enough time to do everything here, it's plenty of time catch some of the area's best offerings.

GETTING THERE

Once you reach Uptown Sedona, some refreshment may be in order. Head to 89A to Oaxaca (928-282-4179; www.oaxacarestaurant.com)—pronounced *wa-HA-ka*. Look for restaurant signage and two arched windows streetside. Take the arched doorway to the right (you'll find a set of stairs) and head upstairs to the restaurant's rooftop cantina, where you can watch the light of the setting sun play off the surrounding red rocks. Sip an aptly named Desert Sunset Margarita (made with prickly pear cactus syrup) and dine on grilled Arizona cactus (marinated, grilled cactus pads served with spicy sauce made of roasted tomatoes, red peppers, chile peppers, and almonds) and an order of guacamole and homemade chips.

For dinner, head back down 89A to just south of the Y, where you'll find Ken's Creekside Restaurant (928-282-1705; www.kenscreekside.com). The menu is full of delightful choices created by owner and award-winning chef Mercer Mohr. And patio seating features spectacular views of the red rocks and Oak Creek, which runs alongside the restaurant.

If you like this . . . keep in mind the restaurant also serves breakfast and lunch.

Sedona doesn't really cater to a late-night crowd (most locations close about 9 or 10 PM); however, Gypsy Lounge at Ken's Creekside features nightly entertainment and a late-night menu ('til midnight). After dinner, grab a seat and a cocktail at Gypsy and listen to live, local music. Sedona is home to

Oaxaca

musicians and singer/songwriters; depending on the night, you may catch jazz or Latin American music, and either might call you for a spin on the dance floor.

DAY 1

Take a Hike

Most places don't open very early in Sedona, so you'll have plenty of time to sneak in a hike. For a quick, easy trip, try one of Sedona's vortex hikes. Bell Rock, one of Sedona's most recognizable landmarks, is located just off AZ 179 as part of the Coconino National Forest. You'll see the bell-shaped rock rising up along the east side of the highway. Pull off at mile marker 309.8 to park. You will need a Red Rock Pass, since you're parking on national forest land. No worries; you can pick up weekly and daily passes at the kiosk in the parking lot. (See *Outdoor Adventures* for more information.) Once you're there, a short path will take you from the lot and up onto the rocks. You can either wander up the sides of Bell Rock or take the Bell Rock Pathway (www.fs.fed.us/r3 /coconino/recreation/red_rock/bell-rock -pathway.shtml), an easy to moderate 3.5-mile hike that will take about two and a half hours to complete.

If you like this . . . consider the 4-mile Courthouse Butte Loop, adjacent to Bell Rock. You can pick it up at the Bell Rock Pathway kiosk, where it parallels the Bell Rock Pathway.

Lunch

For lunch, grab a table window-side (or on the patio, if there's room) at Canyon Breeze (928-282-2112; www.canyon-breeze.com). From your seat, see if you can find Snoopy Rock and Lucy. These red rock formations, named for the famous Peanuts characters because they really do look like them, are easy to see from the 120-foot wall of floor-to-ceiling windows. The restaurant's extensive menu offers a number of choices, from soups, salads, and smoothies to pizzas, burgers, and sandwiches.

Afternoon Sight-Seeing

Well positioned on 89A, Canyon Breeze gives you a great starting point for an afternoon in Uptown Sedona, where you can easily spend half a day wandering from shop to gallery to boutique. You'll find novelty shops (check out the red dirt shirts!); art galleries;

Quick tip: Be aware of the time limits on parking along AZ 89A; you can get a ticket for exceeding the limit (note any chalk marks on your back tire). Also, there is additional parking behind the stores that line 89A.

jewelry, home decor, fudge, and chocolate shops; and touristy little stops that are great for picking up last-minute souvenirs. Take time to have a cup of coffee or iced tea on one of the restaurant or café patios. The views are spectacular. In Uptown, you can take the Sedona Trolley (928-282-4211; www.sedonatrolley.com) for a 55-minute tour of the city or the Seven Canyons; pick up one of several Jeep tours, from A Day in the West and Red Rock Jeep Tours (see *Outdoor Adventures*) to Pink Jeep Tours (see *Day Two*); or

Bell Rock is an iconic Sedona landmark

Javelinas on parade in Uptown Sedona

simply stroll along and enjoy the number of public artworks you'll find along the way (how many colorful javelina can you find?).

Dinner

Situated on Oak Creek at the L'Auberge de Sedona resort, L'Auberge Restaurant (928-282-1661 or 800-272-6777; www.lauberge .com) is an award-winning restaurant serving French-infused American cuisine creek side. You would be hard-pressed to find a more romantic location in all of Arizona. Choose a place on the terrace or in the window-lined dining room overlooking the creek. The seasonal menu changes daily, and the six-course dinner tasting menu is worth consideration. Wine lovers rejoice: the restaurant is a many-time winner of *Wine Spectator* magazine's coveted Best of Award of Excellence.

DAY 2

Breakfast

Your Sedona trip wouldn't be complete without a visit to what locals consider the best breakfast place in town—Coffee Pot Restaurant (928-282-6626; www.coffeepotsedona.com). They open at 6 AM, giving you plenty of time to peruse the menu of 101 omelets that will make all of your breakfast dreams come true (from peanut butter and jelly to Italian sausage and cheese) and still get to your Jeep tour on time.

Take a Ride

Serving Sedona visitors since 1960, Pink Jeep Tours (800-873-3662; www .pinkjeeptours.com) provides more than 10 off-road adventures through the surrounding wilderness areas. Experience the geological, historical,

The view from Submarine Rock

and archaeological treasures that Sedona has to share with these award-winning excursions. Make reservations in advance for their most popular trip: Broken Arrow, a two-hour, 100 percent off-road roller-coaster of a ride that will have you holding on for dear life and most likely screaming (at least a little) with sheer joy as you ride up . . . and down . . . some of the most heart-stopping off-road trails, exploring Submarine Rock and Chicken Point in Munds Mountain Wilderness Area. You'll discover why Chicken Point is called Chicken Point (and I'm not going to ruin it by telling you). This trip is well worth it, full of countless photo opportunities and numerous panoramic views your camera simply won't be able to capture.

Lunch Before You Go

After your hair-raising off-road ride and before you head out of town, stop for lunch at Arizona favorite Javelina Cantina (928-203-9514; www.javelina cantina.com/Sedona) at Hillside Sedona. You can drink in some more of the red rock views from the patio before you head back home. The menu features Baja-inspired Mexican fare—pork, chicken, beef, and seafood tacos; quesadillas; and burritos. If you have time, you're also in the right place for a little last-minute shopping.

Extend Your Stay

If you have more time, try these great places to see and things to do . . .

ARIZONA HERITAGE

Jordan Historical Park (www.sedona museumorg/orchards.html), established in the late 1920s as the Jordan farmstead, is an old apple orchard once operated by Walter and Ruth Jordan.

The property, now listed on the National Register of Historic Places, features a 1929 tractor shed, a 1931 red rock cabin, and a fruit-packing warehouse built in 1947. In 1991 Sedona purchased the last of the land that made up the original farmstead and established the Jordan Historical Park in conjunction with the Sedona Historical Society. The city leases the property to the historical society and the Sedona Heritage Museum (928-282-7038; www.sedonamuseum.org), which highlights pioneer history, movies made in Sedona, and cowboy life, and preserves vintage machinery, the original orchard, and a nature trail.

ARTS & CULTURE

Sedona has a rich artistic community, with numerous art studios and galleries dotting the hillsides. Major events include the annual three-day Sedona International Film Festival (www .sedonafilm.org) and Sedona Jazz on

the Rocks (www.sedonajazz.com), a three-day event that attracts more than five thousand jazz lovers annually.

Located in Hillside Sedona off AZ 179, the Gallery of Modern Masters (928-282-3313 or 888-282-3313; www.galleryofmodernmasters.com) features one of the largest collections of 20th-century modern masters' work in Arizona, including sculptures, hand-blown glass, photography, oils, and ceramics. You will find works by masters Salvador Dalí, Henry Moore, and Pablo Picasso, as well contemporary pieces by ceramist Michel Gustavson, photographers Keoki Flagg and Ian Whitehead, and mixed-media artist Dominique Caron, among others. The gallery also hosts events such as Art, Wine and Talk Receptions.

Sedona Arts Center (928-282-3809 or 888-954-4442; www.sedona artscenter.com), the oldest arts organization in northern Arizona, offers more than 250 classes and workshops, and hosts special events and a revolving arts exhibit. Located just past Uptown

The red rock views from Chicken Point

Sedona on Art Barn Road, the center includes the Members Art Gallery, featuring new monthly exhibits/sales by local artists, and hosts a First Friday Artwalk exhibit and wine reception.

Chapel of the Holy Cross (www .chapeloftheholycross.com) is probably one of the most iconic elements of Sedona. Perched atop the red rocks just off AZ 179, the chapel is a stunning tribute to the mixture of spirituality and art in Sedona.

OUTDOOR ADVENTURES

One Sedona tour guide said on a recent trip, "expect to be outside." The fresh air and natural beauty of the area begs visitors to step outside and enjoy all it has to offer—and Sedona offers quite a lot.

Located in the heart of the Coconino National Forest and bordered on the east and north by Munds Mountain Wilderness Area and Red Rock–Secret Mountain Wilderness Area, respectively, the Sedona area is crisscrossed with more than 100 trails of varying degrees of difficulty. There are also several parks and recreational areas, including Red Rock State Park, Crescent Moon Recreation Park, Posse Grounds Park, and Slide Rock State Park.

Keep in mind that a Red Rock Pass is necessary when parking on Forest Service land. You can pick up one of these passes at either of the two sporting outfitters in town, as well as many of the resorts, hotels, grocery stores, and visitors centers in the area. You can also purchase passes online at www.publiclands.org or via telephone (with Visa or MasterCard) by calling one of the following offices: South Gateway (928-284-5324 or 928-284-5322), Verde Ranger District (928-567-4121), Peaks Ranger District (928-

526-0866), or the Coconino National Forest Supervisor's Office (928-527-3600). For more information about where to pick up a Red Rock Pass, visit www.redrockcountry.org.

Resources for outdoor adventurers include the Red Rock Ranger District (www.fs.fed.us/r3/coconino/recreation/red_rock/rec_redrock.shtml), Coconino National Forest (928-203-7500 or 928-282-4119; www.redrockcountry.org), and the South Gateway Visitor Center (928-284-5323).

Biking

Sedona begs you to spend your time outdoors, and mountain bikers and ATV enthusiasts can find a number of adventurous spots to conquer, including the Bell Rock Pathway. However, be aware that bikes are not allowed in specially designated wilderness areas (Munds Mountain Wilderness Area and Red Rock Secret Wilderness Area)—only in the national forest proper. Also, keep in mind that a Red Rock Pass is required for parking on national forest land. See *Hiking* for more information about trails.

Birding

According to the Northern Arizona Audubon Society (www.nazas.org), Sedona's elevation, changing seasons, and rich riparian areas support a varied population of birds—and thus good birding year-round. Depending on the season, you may find neotropical birds or waterfowl as they migrate through the area to more comfortable climes. Top birding spots in the Sedona area include Red Rock State Park (928-282-6907; www.azparks.gov/Parks /parkhtml/redrock.html) and Oak Creek Canyon. Additional information is available at the Red Rock Ranger District Visitor Contact Center (928-203-2900; www.redrockcountry.org), which is located just south of the Village of Oak Creek on AZ 179.

Camping

A number of popular camping sites in the area offer hiking, biking, fishing, climbing, horseback riding, swimming, wading, birding, photography, wildlife-watching, and picnicking, and allow tent camping, camp trailers, and recreational vehicles. Red Rock Passes are necessary for parking on national forest lands; the cost for a campsite is $15–20 per night, and fees apply for any additional vehicles. Only cash and Arizona checks are accepted. Some sites tend to get quite crowded on weekends, and only about half of the sites take reservations, including Manzanita, Chavez Crossing Group Site, Pine Flat, and Cave Springs campgrounds. Nonreservation sites include Bootlegger, Beaver Creek, and Clear Creek Camp and Group Site campgrounds. Most sites do not have utility hookups and have a

maximum stay of seven days. To be safe, always keep your pets leashed and restrained; do not carry glass containers onto Forest Service land; and, as always, bring plenty of water. For more information about camping in the region, visit www.redrockcountry.org and click on "Recreational Activities."

Hiking

For the best information on directions to trailheads, trail length, and difficulty, consult the Coconino National Forest Web site at www.redrockcountry.org; click on "Maps & Brochures." The available PDF map offers complete listing of trailheads and trails within the Coconino National Forest; for specific information about trails, click on "Recreational Activities" and then "Trails" for a complete list, including distance, difficulty, elevation, and uses. Popular routes include the easy Bell Rock Pathway (3 miles one-way). Both bikers and hikers are welcome on this

Map your route at Bell Rock Pathway

smooth, wide trail that parallels AZ 179; you can pick up two trailheads, Bell Rock Vista and Little Horse, at mileposts 307.5 and 309.4, respectively. Baldwin/Templeton/Cathedral Rock (2 miles one-way) allows you to catch views of Cathedral Rock and Wilson Mountain along a trail that also accesses Oak Creek. Pick up the trailhead at the end of Verde Valley School Road off 179. Jim Thompson Trail (2.4 miles one-way) is easily accessible from Park Ridge Road, which starts off as Jordan Road in Uptown Sedona.

Moderate trails like Devils Bridge (0.9 mile one-way)—which climbs 400 feet to a natural rock arch—offer a steeper climb with great views (and spectacular pictures). The Devils Bridge Trailhead is accessible 1.5 miles down FR 152. Similarly, the Jordan Trail (off Park Ridge Road) is a 2-mile loop with a 200-foot climb. This trail leads to a huge sinkhole called Devil's Kitchen in the Soldier Pass area. For an almost 4-mile loop, try Courthouse Butte Loop. This 250-foot climb is a gentle one as the trail sweeps around Bell Rock and Courthouse Butte at the edge of the Munds Mountain Wilderness Area. Catch the trailhead off 179 in the Village of Oak Creek at the Bell Rock Pathway kiosk. The Brins Mesa Trail, which was severely damaged during the 2005 fire that swept through area, is a 3-mile (one-way) trail with a 600-foot change in elevation. The climb is worth it—you end up on a flat mesa with panoramic views of Sedona and the awe-inspiring 2,000-foot-high Mogollon Rim; hikers share this path with horseback riders. The trail is accessible from Park Ridge/Jordan Road in Uptown and is intersected by the Soldier Pass Trail.

For a difficult hike and a 2,300-

Courthouse Butte

foot climb, conquer the Wilson Mountain Trail (5.6 miles one-way). This all-day trek can be started at Midgely Bridge off AZ 89A. As with all physical activity in Arizona, it's important to stay hydrated. Bring plenty of water, and let someone know where you're going and when you plan to return.

The views are spectacular and, once you get in among the trees, it's surprisingly quiet.

Jeep Tours

In addition to Pink Jeep Tours (see *48 Hours*), local Jeep tour companies include Red Rock Jeep Tours (928-282-6826; www.redrockjeep.com), which offers a helicopter/Jeep combo tour, and A Day in the West Jeep Tours (928-282-4320 or 800-973-3662; www.adayinthewest.com), which has guides decked out in their best Western gear. (Or, if you prefer your horse-power with legs, the latter offers horseback-riding tours.)

Tour guides add the pizzazz to any trip, recommending where to point your camera, when to hang on, and how the red rock formations got their names. A 15 percent gratuity is recommended. Also recommended are reservations, though it is possible to walk in and jump right in a Jeep. Most companies require a two-person minimum and 24 hours for cancellations. Be sure to wear lots of sunscreen (bring extra), a hat, sunglasses, and comfortable shoes. And don't forget your camera!

Parks

Red Rock State Park (928-282-6907; www.azparks.gov/Parks/parkhtml/redro ck.html) features several trail options that parallel Oak Creek and link to the national forest. Access it off Red Rock Loop Road from AZ 89A; it's about 7 miles north of Sedona. There is a $5-per-car fee year-round. Red Rock State

Park offers opportunities for recreational and educational experiences; call 928-282-6907 for details. Red Rock State Park escaped closure in 2010 and is now open daily from 8–5.

Slide Rock State Park (928-282-3034; www.pr.state.az.us/Parks/park html/sliderock.html), in the heart of Oak Creek Canyon, is a favorite spot on hot summer days; it features a natural water slide that kids (and adults)

Pink Jeep Tours

Playing in a creek at Oak Creek Canyon

Photo courtesy Jacqueline Kinsella

can't get enough of. Originally part of the 43-acre Pendley homestead and apple farm, today the park is on the National Register of Historic Places and features wading, fishing, hiking, swimming, and bird-watching. There's a $10 fee per vehicle (one to four adults) and a $2 charge per individual from Memorial Day weekend through Labor Day weekend.

Zoos

Out of Africa (928-567-2842; www.out ofafricapark.com), originally sited in the Phoenix metropolitan area, relocated several years ago to the Verde Valley. Get up close and personal with some of Africa's people-friendly animals, and watch from behind fences as brave trainers work with the more dangerous predators. This park offers a unique and informative animal encounter. Tiger Splash is quite an experience—watch as trainers and tigers play in the water.

SHOPPING & SPAS

There are several main shopping districts/areas in Sedona, including Tlaquepaque, on AZ 179 just south of the Y; Uptown Sedona (turn right at the Y off 179); Hillside, on AZ 179 south of Tlaquepaque Village; and the shops in West Sedona (turn left onto 89A from AZ 179).

Hillside Sedona (928-282-4500; www.hillsidesedona.net) is well known for its collection of art galleries, restaurants, and specialty shops. Galleries include the Gallery of Modern Masters and The Lost Woodsman Studio (406-544-2283; www.rowleydesigns.com), gallery of master sculptor Rick J. Rowley. Restaurants like Arizona favorite Shugrue's Hillside Grill (928-282-

5300; www.shugrues.com/hsg), specialty shops, wine tasting, and home decor shops round out this experience of some of Sedona's finest.

Built in the mid-1970s, Tlaquepaque Arts & Crafts Village (928-282-4838; www.tlaq.com)—pronounced *TLA-keh-PAH-keh*—was designed in the tradition of Mexican artisans and builders, incorporating plazas, fountains and verandas, ironwork, handpainted tiles, and plenty of shady spaces beneath a thick canopy of cottonwood and sycamore trees. The vision of Abe Miller, this Spanish-style arts village hosts a variety of boutiques, galleries, and specialty shops, as well as five restaurants. Named after a suburb of Guadalajara, Mexico, Tlaquepaque features Western, traditional, and contemporary art and sculpture, including works in bronze, clay, paper, wood, and stone, as well as Southwest photography; also look for decorative rugs, handmade Andean arts and crafts, clothing, paintings, quilts, decorative glass, jewelry, bath products, candles, seasonal decor, and pottery.

Restaurants include El Rincon Restaurante Mexicano (928-282-4648; www.elrinconrestaurant.com), serving Arizona-style Mexican cuisine; Oak Creek Brewery and Grill (928-282-3300; www.oakcreekpub.com), with American grill fare and beers brewed on-site; and Secret Garden Café (928-203-9564; www.sedonasecretgardencafe.com), which serves gourmet soups, salads, and coffees.

Located in Uptown Sedona and set against an enchanting red rock backdrop, Sedona Center (928-282-4527; www.sedona-center.com) will meet your shopping, hiking, dining, and even lodging needs (the Amara Hotel is located here). You

Tlaquepaque Arts & Crafts Village

Sedona Spirit

Visitors and residents alike wonder about what makes Sedona unique—the metaphysical power of its vortexes, the intense electromagnetic energy caused by the oxidized iron (the red in the rocks), or simply beautiful views and clear air. Wherever the power originates, most agree that visiting Sedona is an inspiring event. That's why so many come back—or even stay. Amplify the intensity of your experience with a yoga hike, vortex tour, or four-day retreat led by Johanna Mosca, PhD, and the team at **Sedona Spirit Yoga & Hiking** (928-282-9900; www.yogalife.net). Mosca, the author of the book *Cultivate Contentment,* leads her guests on simultaneously physical and spiritual journeys among the red rocks in Sedona or at her retreat house just outside of Sedona.

In Sedona there are four **vortexes;** considered to be areas with a high concentration of positive metaphysical energy, they are believed to offer restorative properties to those who visit them. You'll often see individuals meditating or performing yoga poses at these locations. One of the easiest to get to is Bell Rock, which is said to have high levels of energy surrounding it. One indicator of these energy fields is said to be the twisted tree trunks you'll find along the path. Several tour operators offer vortex-specific excursions, including Sedona Spirit Yoga & Hiking, Red Rock Jeep Tours (see *48 Hours*), and **Retreat and Heal** (928-282-5237; www.retreatandheal.com), which offers spiritual and wellness retreats, including spiritual vortex tours, health spa services, intuitive readings, and hypnotherapy for women and couples. Day spas such as **Sedona's New Day Spa** (928-282-7502; www.sedonanewdayspa.com) feature both traditional massages and New Age readings and energy-balancing treatments.

Twisted trees covered in red rock dust

Fast fact: Sedona is unique in that it has four vortexes or energy fields: Bell Rock, Airport Mesa, Red Rock Crossing/Cathedral Rock, and Boynton Canyon (near the Kachina Woman red rock formation in Boynton Canyon).

Sedona is also home to a number of psychics, hypnotherapists, and spiritualists who offer their services among the restorative and healing energy of the surrounding red rocks. Psychics like **Claudia Coronado** (928-300-2112; www.claudiacoronado.com) offer psychic readings to help you chuck your emotional baggage, shed a former skin, or connect with your spiritual self, and medical intuitives like Deena Lee of **Sedona Healing & Hypnotherapy** (928-282-9777; www.deenalee.com) offer alternative methods of healing.

Quick tip: Take home a piece of Sedona. More than your traditional T-shirt, Red Rock Original shirts are bathed in the red dirt Sedona is so famous for. You'll find them at Cheers (800-658-5742; www.cheer sofsedona.com).

will find more than 30 boutique-style shops offering an array of items, including jewelry, art, and home decor. There are three restaurants, including the Hundred Rox at Amara Hotel (see *Local Flavors*), and the Canyon Breeze Restaurant and Bar (928-282-2112; www.canyon-breeze.com), which serves coffee, smoothies, pizza, sandwiches, and salads. Grab a table beside one of the picture windows for a relaxing and warmer (during winter)

experience of the surrounding beauty; on balmier days, sit on the outdoor patio.

The Shops at Hyatt Piñon Pointe (www.theshopsathyattpinonpointe.com) comprises more than 20 stores, galleries, and restaurants, all just north of the Y in Uptown Sedona. The open courtyard setting and patio seating offer spectacular views of the surrounding red rock formations, and you'll find works of art along the walkways. Restaurants include Arizona favorite Wildflower Bread Company (928-204-2223; www.wildflowerbread .com), for wonderful soups, salads, and sandwiches; Hiro Sushi (928-282-0992; www.hirosedona.com), for fabulous Japanese cuisine and fresh sushi; and The Art of Wine (877-903-WINE; www.artowine.com), for Arizona wine and daily wine tastings.

Side Trips

ROAMING THE DESERT

APACHE TRAIL: AZ 88 FROM TORTILLA FLAT TO ROOSEVELT DAM

The Apache Trail—used as early as A.D. 900 by the Salado Indians as a footpath through the mountains, and later expanded to facilitate the building of the Roosevelt Dam in the early 20th century—wanders through some of the state's most beautiful desert terrain. It is best seen from a tour van with a knowledgeable guide pointing out exactly where to feast your eyes. A novice tourist can get lost in the breathtaking beauty along the trail.

This narrow dirt road hugs the mountain walls as it dips and spirals through lush canyons, above sparkling blue lakes, and amid saguaro forests from Roosevelt Lake in the Mazatzal Mountains through the Superstition Wilderness to AZ 88 at Tortilla Flat. The view is awe inspiring, and some of the hairpin turns are downright spine tingling—a disastrous combination for a curious driver. Consider leaving the driving to a tour company and gorge yourself on one stunning view after another. Not only will they keep you safely on the road, but they'll point out the various desert floras, both native and transplant; recite the local lore; and tell you where to point and when to click the camera. Ask in advance where the best seat is to take pictures out your window—it will be worth it!

Roosevelt Dam, north end of the Apache Trail

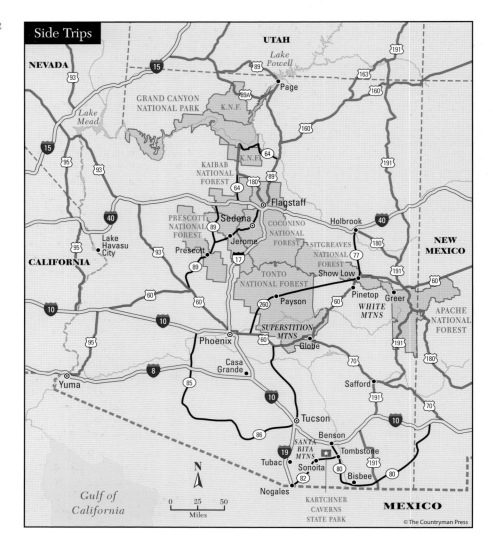

Side Trips

Roosevelt Lake at Tonto National Monument

The unpaved Apache Trail hugs cliff sides as it wends its way through the Superstition Mountains and Tonto National Forest

Tortilla Flat

Located about 18 miles northeast of Apache Junction on AZ 88, Tortilla Flat (www.tortillaflataz.com) was built in 1904 as a rest stop along the Apache Trail and now has a total population of maybe six people. But this little one-horse town knows how to serve up a good time. The walls of its only restaurant and bar are covered in dollar bills from visitors. Grab a saddle (the seat of the bar stools), order a cold draft and a juicy burger, and listen to the live entertainment out on the patio. Wander next door to the Country Store and Ice Cream Shop for dessert. The town sits above Canyon Lake on the Apache Trail.

Superstition Mountains

The Superstition Mountains—aptly named—comprise 160,000 acres cloaked in 9,000 years of mystery. Archaeological studies indicate that the area was inhabited some 7,000 years B.C.; more recent inhabitants have included the Salado and Hohokam, who lived here until the mid-15th century, when they mysteriously abandoned the area, and the Apache, who arrived about the same time. More recent mysteries include the legend of the Lost Dutchman Mine. Legend holds that a miner named Jacob Waltz, known locally as the Dutchman, discovered a gold mine in the mid- to late 19th century; he never told anyone where it was, however, and his partner met with an untimely death. So the secret went with Jacob to his grave in 1891. And though many treasurer hunters have searched—and some have even died trying—not a single person has ever found the lost mine or the gold.

To get a feel for the mysteries of the mountains and its former mining life and applicable lore, visit Superstition Mountain Museum (480-983-4888; ww .superstitionmountainmuseum.org). Or take a trip yourself through the Superstition Wilderness Area (480-610 -3300; www.fs.fed.us/r3/tonto/wilderness /wilderness-superstitionindex.shtml),

Quick tip: Be sure to stick to designated trails, bring plenty of water, and wear sunscreen. Be prepared for significant temperature changes even in warmer months; the days may be hot, but evenings can cool quickly once the sun sets. Tell someone where you're going and when you expect to return.

house was used to chart the stars; others believe it was the home of the tribe's most revered elders.

BISBEE

The once booming mining town of Bisbee (www.discoverbisbee.com or www.city ofbisbee.com) is now a quiet little artists' colony ensconced in its past. Established in 1880 to support the Copper Queen Mine and named after one of the mine's financial backers—Judge Dewitt Bisbee—this town, in its heyday, provided the infrastructure for 20,000 people. Cool off with a tour through the Copper Queen Mine (520-432-2071 or 866-432-2071; www.queenminetour.com), which produced almost 3 million ounces of gold and more than 8 billion pounds of copper in almost a century of operation. In that time its miners scraped, shoveled, drilled, and hauled more than $6 billion worth of ore from its depths. Closed in the mid-1970s when it began losing its profitability, the mine reopened in 1976 as a tour. Don a hard hat, lantern, and yellow slicker; hop on the mine train; and head 1,500 feet underground, where it's 47 degrees Fahrenheit year-round. Or take the Van Tours of Historic Bisbee & Surface Mines (520-432-2071 or 866-432-207; www.amdest.com/az/bisbee/queenmine.html). This one-and-a-quarter-hour tour focuses on the tales of old Bisbee. Guides point out top spots like the mining mansions, the Lavender Pit (it swallowed a neighborhood whole about 50 years ago), and the historic district, including such famous haunts as the Copper Queen Hotel (520-432-2216; www.copperqueen.com), which opened in 1902, and continues to operate more than a century later.

TUCSON

With a population topping 1 million in 2007, Tucson (888-2-TUCSON; www.visit tucson.org) is Arizona's second-largest city and home to ASU's archrival, University of Arizona. (It's a friendly competition that may have started when Phoenix won the bid to serve as state capital.) While both cities embody the informality of the Old West, Tucson may be more relaxed and content with its origins. Nicknamed the Old Pueblo for the presidio that marks its place in territorial and border history, Tucson—rich with Native American, Spanish, and Mexican influences—was founded a good hundred years before Phoenix. It's bordered by four mountain ranges: the Tucson Mountains to the west, Rincon on the south, Santa Catalina on the north, and Santa Rita to the east. Stunning views abound from mountaintop vistas as well as street corners and highways. This southern city's desert beauty is perhaps the greatest part of its charm.

The Arizona State Museum (520-621-6302; www.statemuseum.arizona .edu), a Smithsonian Institution affiliate, was founded in 1893. As the oldest and largest anthropology museum in the Southwest, it is home to the largest whole-vessel collection of Southwest Indian pottery in the world. Past

Quick tip: To get to the Arizona State Museum from I-10, take Speedway Boulevard east to Euclid Avenue. Turn south onto Euclid and proceed to the parking facilities. You can use the uncovered lot at Tyndall and Second, only a block away, but there is a fee on weekdays. Parking is free on weekends.

exhibits include Set in Stone: 2000 Years of Gem and Mineral Trade in the Southwest, which highlighted Native American jewelry then and now, as well as the prominence of turquoise—Arizona's state gem.

Plane lovers rejoice. The Pima Air and Space Museum (520-618-4815; www.pimaair.org) is the largest aircraft museum in the West. More than 250 aircraft, including bombers, fighter planes, transports, and civil and NASA vessels, call the PASM home. You'll find exhibits following the history of air travel from the Wright brothers to NASA, as well as the historical significance of aircraft and their personnel.

If you like this . . . try the the Aerospace Maintenance and Regeneration Center (AMARC) or "boneyard" located on the Davis-Monthan Air Force Base. To tour this facility (for an additional $6 fee), contact 520-574-0462 and ask for the reservation desk; reservations are strongly recommended.

Hour-and-a-half docent-led walking tours will take you through exhibits in Hangars 1, 3, and 4. These tours are free with admission; call for times. You can also take a one-hour tram tour ($5 fee) narrated by a docent—many of whom have experience with the planes you'll see. On this ride among the museum's outdoor 160-plus-aircraft display, you'll see three huge B-52 bombers, an SR-71 Blackbird, and much more.

> **Quick tip:** To reach the Pima Air and Space Museum from I-10, take the Valencia Road exit (on the south end of Tucson) and continue about 2 miles to the entrance.

For some, the name DeGrazia is synonymous with Tucson and even the Southwest. Ettore "Ted" DeGrazia, born in 1909 in the small mining camp of Morenci in eastern Arizona, was the son of a miner who went on to become one of the Southwest's best-known and most beloved artists. After his works appeared in *Arizona Highways* in 1941, and inspired by the praise of Diego Rivera and José Clemente, with whom he'd worked in Mexico, DeGrazia earned three degrees, including a master's of arts from University of Arizona. His bright, whimsical paintings and sketches of children, angels, and Southwestern figures have been reproduced throughout the world on greeting cards, calendars, ornaments, and prints.

DeGrazia Gallery in the Sun (520-299-9191 or 800-545-2185; www.degrazia.org) was designed by Southwest artist Ted DeGrazia in the 1950s and built with the help of Native American friends proficient at making adobe brick. The 10-acre spot, nestled in the foothills of the Catalina Mountains on Swan Road north of Sunrise Drive, includes the artist's home and studio, as well as a small gallery and a larger gallery built in 1965. Today a collection of 15,000 original works, including oils, watercolors, sketches, and sculptures, revolves around a permanent exhibit of six paintings depicting Native cultures and historic events of the Southwest. In 2006 the Gallery in the Sun Historic District was added to the National Register of Historic Places.

The Arizona–Sonora Desert Museum (520-883-2702; www.desert museum.org) in Tucson offers a one-of-a-kind look at the Sonoran Desert and its natural inhabitants. Along 2 miles of paths and across 21 acres of the Sonoran Desert, you will find mountain lions, prairie dogs, gila monsters, javelinas, and rattlesnakes among the three hundred animal species that call this combination zoo, natural history museum, and botanical garden home. More than a thousand kinds of desert flora will expand your sense of the desert, which is greener and prettier than you might expect.

See the desert in all of its glory at the Saguaro National Park (Rincon Mountain District Visitor Center, 520-733-5153; www.nps.gov/sagu). The national park straddles Tucson, with the Rincon Mountain District to the east, the Tucson Mountain District to the west. The park is excellent for biking. Try the paved, 8-mile Cactus Forest Loop Drive in the Rincon, or the gravel, 6-mile Bajada Loop Drive through the Tucson Mountains.

> **Quick tip:** The Arizona–Sonora Desert Museum is mostly outdoors, and walking is required to see the sights.

> **Quick tip:** Bring plenty of water when visiting Saguaro N.P.; you can fill up at either of the visitors centers in the park. Pit toilets are available at all picnic areas. Bring ID and emergency contact information. Helmets are required for anyone bicycling (passengers, too) under the age of 18; however, they are recommended for all bicyclists. After dark you must have a rear reflector and a headlight. Bicyclists are required to obey all traffic laws and signals.

To reach the Rincon Mountain District, take I-10 to exit 275 (Houghton Road); drive 9.5 miles north to Old Spanish Trail and turn right. Continue 3 miles southeast to the park entrance on the left side of the road.

For the Tucson Mountain District, take I-10 to exit 242 (Avra Valley Road), drive 5 miles west to Sandario Road, and turn left. Proceed 9 miles south to Kinney Road; turn left. After 2 more miles the visitors center is on your left.

PAYSON

Enjoy cooler weather and ponderosa pines just 90 minutes from the Valley: at 5,000 feet, Payson (www.ci.payson.az.us) is a year-round retreat for Valley residents. The town celebrates its Western heritage with events like "the World's Oldest Continuous Rodeo," the Old-Time Fiddlers' State Championship, and the Bluegrass Festival. Natural attractions include Tonto Natural Bridge and the Mogollon Rim. Tonto Natural Bridge (520-476-4202), which is 13 miles northwest of Payson off AZ 87, is a 400-foot-wide natural travertine bridge that is considered the world's largest of its kind. It spans Pine Creek 183 feet above the water; trails and paths offer various scenic views of the bridge.

JEROME

Clinging to the side of Cleopatra Hill in the Prescott National Forest is the city of Jerome (www.jeromechamber.com)—a town that, in its heyday, was the toast of investors. Today it is a crumbling, though charming, artists' retreat—a ghost town clinging to its mortal body. You will find shops, galleries, and restaurants interspersed with condemned structures, empty basements where buildings once stood, and a jailhouse that slid down the side of the mountain. While the miners pulled billions of dollars' worth of copper, gold, and silver out of the hundreds of miles of tunnels beneath Jerome, the land above hiccupped and rocked, shattering windows, shifting foundations, and moving the town down the mountainside inches at a time. After 75 years of mining, operations ceased in 1953, and the population dropped from 15,000 at its peak in the 1920s to 50 people. In 1976 Jerome became a National Historic Landmark.

Among the ruins and bed & breakfasts, you will find plaques relating the history of the city, shops such as the Jerome Historical Society's Mine Museum & Gift Shop (928-634-5477; www.jeromehistoricalsociety.com), and a thriving artists' community. Check out the Flatiron Café (928-634-2733; www.flatironcafejerome .com) for breakfast and lunch or Belgian Jennie's Bordello Bistro & Pizzeria (928-639-3141; 412 Main Street) for pizza and pasta. The Jerome Grand Hotel (928-634-8200; www.jeromegrandhotel.net) was once the town hospital and is now a charming hotel with unbelievable views of the Verde Valley and Sedona; its restaurant, the Asylum (928-639-3197; www.theasylum.biz), is one of only 2,800 restaurants worldwide to be given the *Wine Spectator* Award of Excellence. You'll find a sophisticated menu with a Southwest twist—like the roasted butternut squash soup or prickly pear BBQ pork tenderloin. Don't forget the numerous shops, boutiques, and art galleries lining Main Street and Clark Street. For dinner and a movie the old-fashioned way—a chuckwagon meal and stage show on the Verde River—try Blazin' M Ranch Western Dinner Theater (928-634-0334 or 800-937-8643; www.blazinm.com), just down the mountain in Cottonwood.

The steep streets of mining-town-turned-artist-colony Jerome

I'll Have a Taste of That

Jackie Dishner

First, Sonoita did it. Willcox followed. Now the Verde Valley has hold of Arizona's wine industry and won't let go.

Since Maynard James Keenan (front man for the rock band Tool, and an Arizona vintner) took his documentary, *Blood into Wine* (www.bloodintowine.com), on the road in February 2010, he's brought a tremendous amount of attention to Arizona wine country, specifically the northern region. But there's more to it than Keenan's celebrity brush with success at his vineyards in the Verde Valley.

In 2006, Arizona was home to 12 wineries, most of them located in the southern part of the state. Then the legislature passed a law that year that opened the market, and boutique wineries prospered. Today, 40 wineries and at least a dozen more in developmental stage exist statewide. For more information, visit www.arizonawine.org.

If you'd like to sample some Arizona wine, try these tasting rooms:

Along the Willcox Wine Trail

Carlson Creek Vineyard (520-766-3000; www.carlsoncreek.com), Willcox. Tastings take place Tuesday–Sunday 11–5. $6 (keep the glass).

Keeling-Schaefer Tasting Room (520-766-0600; www.keelingschaefervineyards.com), Willcox. Tastings take place Thursday–Sunday 11–4. $5 (keep the glass).

Construction for **Gallifant Cellars,** 108 N. Railroad Avenue, Willcox, is under way as of summer 2010, and it's due to open soon.

Along the Verde Valley Wine Trail

Arizona Stronghold (928-639-2789; www.arizonastrongholdvineyards.com), Old Town Cottonwood. Tastings take place Monday, Thursday, and Sunday noon–7, Wednesday noon–5, and Friday–Saturday noon–9. $8 for five tastes (keep the glass).

Pillsbury Wine Company (928-639-0646; www.pillsburywine.com), Old Town Cottonwood. Tastings take place Monday–Thursday 11–6, Friday–Saturday 11–9, Sunday noon–6. $12 for five tastes (keep the glass).

Jackie Dishner is a Phoenix-based writer and author of Backroads & Byways of Arizona, *in which she covers Arizona's wine country.*

FLAGSTAFF

Home to Northern Arizona University and a number of museums, attractions, restaurants, and B&Bs, Flagstaff (928-774-9541 or 800-379-0065; www.flagstaffarizona.org) is worth a visit. From here, you can visit the Grand Canyon, Lake Powell, Sedona, the Navajo and Hopi reservations, and Monument Valley. In town, take time for the Lowell Observatory, Museum of Northern Arizona, the Grand Canyon Railway, Meteor Crater, Riordan Mansion, or the Flagstaff Arizona Snowbowl.

From April through October, you can hike through The Arboretum at Flagstaff (928-774-1442; www.thearb.org), a 200-acre wildflower meadow at 7,000 feet—considered one of the country's largest collection of high-country wildflowers.

At the Arizona Historical Society–Pioneer Museum (928-774-6272; www .arizonahistoricalsociety.org), Flagstaff and northern Arizona's dynamic past has been captured and preserved.

At an elevation of 7,000 feet and with an average snowfall of 260 inches, the Arizona Snowbowl (928-779-1951; snow report 928-779-4577; www.arizonasnow bowl.com) makes winter sports a distinct possibility. Ski mid-December through mid-April 9–4. Summertime (Memorial Day–mid-October) means a scenic sky ride to 11,500 feet (10–4).

Winter or summer, enjoy the quietude of the world's largest contiguous ponderosa pine forest at Coconino National Forest (928-527-3600; www.fs.fed.us /r3/coconino). The ecology changes from desert cactus at 2,600 feet to alpine tundra at more than 12,600 feet.

Arizona is the Grand Canyon state, and Grand Canyon National Park (520-638-7875; www.nps.gov/grca) is a World Heritage Site—a magnificent place that defies all attempts to describe it, one that draws people from all over the world to gawk at, helicopter over, climb into, and raft down. Thus, a trip to the big hole in the ground is strongly recommended; it is something you simply have to see for yourself.

The Grand Canyon—carved by millennia of exposure to the Colorado River and the natural erosion of weather, rain, wind, and time—is the main focus of the park, which encompasses 277 miles of river and adjacent uplands from the southern point of Glen Canyon National Recreation Area to the eastern border of Lake Mead National Recreation Area. Visitors come to take pictures, hike, bike, wander the numerous paths, and browse the exhibits and displays. The South Rim is more accessible to visitors from the Phoenix area; the North Rim is only open mid-May through late October.

If you're planning to spend the night in Flag (as Arizonans like to call it), stay at one of the town's B&Bs, which are charming alternatives to brand hotels. Consider The Inn at 410 Bed and Breakfast (928-774-0088 or 800-774-2008; www .inn410.com), deemed Arizona's best by the *Arizona Republic,* or Starlight Pines Bed and Breakfast (928-527-1912 or 800-752-1912; www.starlightpinesbb.com), considered Flagstaff's most romantic.

Restaurants include Brix (928-213-1021; www.brixflagstaff.com), a charming eatery that serves a wonderful lunch and dinner menu; the extensive wine list offers an array of by-the-glass choices. Cottage Place (928-774-8431; www.cottage place.com), an award-winning establishment of 25 years, serves amazing entrées like scallop sauté en croute, Gorgonzola-encrusted filet, and grilled duck breast.

In the Verde Valley, about 50 miles south of Flagstaff, high above the floodplain of Beaver Creek, lies one of the best-preserved cliff dwellings in North America—Montezuma Castle National Monument (602-567-5276; www.nps .gov/moca). This five-story, 20-room dwelling was built by the Sinagua Indians more than six hundred years ago. Assuming the prehistoric ruins were built by the Aztec emperor Montezuma (who never even visited the structure), early settlers named it Montezuma Castle. The national monument has a museum displaying artifacts found at the site, a short hiking and biking trail, and self-guided tour signs describing the cultural and natural significance of the area. Dogs are allowed on the trail but must be on a leash no longer than 6 feet. Montezuma Castle is located in the Tonto National Forest.

WHITE MOUNTAINS

If you're looking to escape the hot weather altogether, or if you're seeking a white Christmas, the White Mountains are an excellent choice. The towns of Showlow, Pinetop, and Greer have summer cabins, various outdoor activities (fishing, hiking, biking, canoeing, and skiing), and a ranch-style resort. Hidden Meadow Ranch (928-333-1000; www.hiddenmeadow.com), a 150-acre property in Greer, offers its guests cabins instead of hotel rooms. At 8,500 feet above sea level, the resort tends to be pretty busy in the summer as Arizonans escape the heat; in winter, it becomes a winter wonderland. Activities include hiking, canoeing, horseback riding, fly-fishing, skiing, snowboarding, sledding, and ice fishing.

In this area, you'll also find the Apache-Sitgreaves National Forests (www.fs .fed.us/r3/asnf), which together cover more than 2 million acres of mountain land, and the Apache Tribe and several historical and recreational sites, including the Apache Cultural Museum at Fort Apache Park (http://wmat.us/fortapachepark .htm) and Sunrise Park Resort (928-735-7669 or 800-772-7669; www.sunriseski park.com).

PRESCOTT

The first capital of the Arizona Territory, Prescott (www.visit-prescott.com), pronounced *PRESS-kit,* remains steeped in its frontier heritage. Bordered by the Prescott National Forest, "Everybody's Hometown" enjoys four mild seasons and cooler temperatures than the Valley. Its elevation and proximity to the national forest make it an ideal spot for hiking, mountain biking, and horseback riding. You'll also find historical sites, shops featuring local artists, and the infamous Whiskey Row's numerous saloons, including cinematic superstar The Palace Restaurant and Saloon (928-541-1996; www.historicpalace.com), established in 1877 and featured in the film *Junior Bonner* with Steve McQueen, among others. The saloon still has the same 1880s Brunswick Bar that some of the frontier's toughest customers rubbed elbows with.

Two miles east of Cordes Junction, Paolo Soleri's Arcosanti (928-632-7135; www.arcosanti.org), a practice in arcology (architecture and ecology), is still under construction; guests can tour the compound or even stay the night.

Discover art at some of Prescott's cultural institutions: Phippen Art Museum (928-778-1385; www.phippenartmuseum.org) features contemporary and historic art of the American West. Sharlot Hall Museum (928-445-3122; www.sharlot.org) hosts exhibits and artifacts that reveal the stories of Arizona's settlers and supports the Blue Rose Theater, which presents historical dramas. Smoki Museum (928-445-1230; www.smokimuseum.org) has promoted appreciation for Native American culture since 1935 and houses the largest collection of Kate Cory oil paintings in the country. Yavapai College Gallery and Sculpture Garden (928-776-2031; www.yc.edu) features changing exhibits of local, regional, and national artists; the

A view of red rocks from Prescott

Sculpture Garden (www.yc.edu/content/ycf/friends/default.htm) accommodates some interesting contemporary pieces, including a leaping frog, a hammered copper fountain, and a welded family. Finally, enjoy a private tour of 40 years' worth of cinema technology and Arizona film history at Professor Hall's Cinema Museum (928-777-9134; www.silentmovies.com), open by appointment only.

TUBAC

The town of Tubac (www.tubacarizona.com) is located about 50 miles south of Tucson, off I-19 toward Nogales. Given its proximity to the border with Mexico, Tubac played a big part in Spanish, Mexican, and Native American cultures before the area became part of U.S. territory. Originally founded in 1752 by the Spanish to protect the area from the Indians, Tubac's history is now preserved by the Tubac Presidio State Historic Park (520-398-2252; http://azstateparks.com/Parks /TUPR/index.html). Today, Tubac is a small artists colony with art galleries, shops, and boutiques showcasing leatherwork, painting, pottery, clothing, and jewelry, to name a few. It's a pleasant afternoon roaming the dusty streets, perusing the many stores and shops, and visiting with local artists.

Make the historic Tubac Golf Resort & Spa (520-398-2211 or 800-848-7893; www.tubacgolfresort.com), walking distance from Tubac, your home base. The resort occupies 500 acres of land along the Santa Cruz River and includes several historic buildings, including the original residence of Don Otero. The land was originally granted by the Spanish king in 1789 to the Otero family, who built a

Tubac Golf Resort's famous *Tin Cup* golf course

ranching empire that lasted long into the mid-20th century. In 1959, a group of businessmen, including legendary entertainer Bing Crosby, purchased the property.

Today, the resort features the championship golf course seen in the movie *Tin Cup,* which starred Rene Russo and Kevin Costner. The resort features a full-service on-site spa and salon, as well as three on-site restaurants: Dos Silos (named for the old grain silos that still stand on the property); the historic Stables Ranch Grille (which some say is haunted), named as such because it once served as the stables for the property; and La Cantina. The Stables features patio seating complete with stunning views of the golf course, a lounge with patio seating, and live music on Friday nights. The restaurants serve a blend of Southwestern, Mexican, and Spanish cuisine.

Rent a bicycle from the resort's front desk and take a ride along the quiet, winding roads, or schedule a horseback-riding trip with Ride the West (858-270-7432 or 866-454-7433; www.ridethewest.com). Boating and fishing are nearby at Patagonia Lake (520-287-6965; www.pr.state.az.us/Parks/parkhtml/patagonia .html). Also nearby are Fred Lawrence Whipple Observatory (www.cfa.harvard .edu/facilities/flwo), atop Mount Hopkins in the Santa Rita Mountains, and Tumacácori National Historical Park (520-398-2341; www.nps.gov/tuma), site of the San José de Tumacácori Mission, established in 1691.

The resort also serves as an excellent base for a wine tour of southern Arizona. Several vineyards in the area showcase Arizona wines, including Arizona Vineyards (520-287-7972; 1830 Patagonia Highway), in Nogales; Callaghan Vineyards (520-455-5322; www.callaghanvineyards.com), in Elgin; Sonoita Vineyards (520-455-5893; www.sonoitavineyards.com), in Sonoita; and Village of Elgin Winery (520-455-9309; www.elginwines.com), in Elgin.

Quick tip: Walking shoes are required. To reach the Titan Missile Museum from Tucson, take I-19 south toward Green Valley and Nogales. Exit at Duval Mine Road (exit 69), turn west, and follow the signs. The entrance is on the north side of the road, approximately 0.1 mile past the intersection of La Canada and Duval Mine Road.

Located 25 miles south of Tucson, the Titan Missile Museum (520-625-7736; www.titanmissilemuseum.org) is the last of the 54 Titan II Intercontinental Ballistic Missile (ICBM) complexes that were "on alert" during the height of the Cold War. In 1982, a year after President Ronald Reagan announced the disassembly of the missiles, this particular site was ready for deactivation and destruction. A group

Dos Silos Restaurant

of volunteers and the U.S. Air Force collaborated to deactivate the missile and preserve the site as a museum, which opened to the public in 1986. In 1994 the site was named a National Historic Landmark; in 2003 the museum opened the Count Ferdinand von Galen Education and Research Center to preserve missile program artifacts and develop and facilitate the museum's educational mission. The tour includes a six-story view of the Titan II missile in its silo, a visit to the underground launch control center, and a simulated missile launch.

San José de Tumacácori at Tumacácori National Historical Park

Also nearby, in Benson, is Kartchner Caverns (520-586-2283; http://azstate parks.com/Parks/KACA). Considered a "live" cave, the limestone cavern, discovered in 1974, is interspersed with both stalagmites, which grow up from the floor of the cave, and stalactites, which drip down and hang like icicles from the roof of the cave. Because water continues to drip throughout the cave, these formations continue to "grow," creating a visually stunning subterranean landscape. The guided tour lasts one and a half hours.

If you like this . . . try **Colossal Cave** *(520-647-7275; www.colossalcave .com), just outside Tucson, for a 50-minute tour of the cave and its history and geological significance.*

Information
LOCAL RESOURCES

Photo courtesy Jacqueline Kinsella

AMBULANCE, FIRE & POLICE

For emergency help in the Valley, dial 911 or 0 for an operator.

Poison Control: 602-253-3334
Center for Prevention of Abuse and Violence (CASA): 602-254-6400
National Sexual Assault Hotline: 800-656-HOPE

Arizona Department of Public Safety (www.azdps.gov), P.O. Box 6638, Phoenix, AZ 85005).

Highway Patrol (main switchboard 602-223-2000; road conditions 888-411-7623).

Arizona Counter Terrorism Information Center (ACTIC) (602-644-5805 or 877-2-SAVEAZ).

Maricopa County Sheriff's Office (Sheriff Joe Arpaio, 602-876-1801; Chiefs and Commanders, 602-876-1801; www.mcso.org), 100 W. Washington, Suite 1900, Phoenix.

Phoenix Police Department Information Desk (602-262-7626; no reports or dispatch).

Emergency Management
Arizona Department of Emergency Management (602-244-0504 or 877-240-9735; www.dem.state.az.us).

Maricopa County—Emergency Management (602-273-1411; www.maricopa .gov/emerg_mgt), 2035 N. 52nd St., Phoenix.

City of Phoenix Emergency Management Program (602-495-2077; www.ci .phoenix.az.us/EMERGENCYMGMT/index.html).

Nonemergency Police Numbers

Phoenix: 602-262-6151

Scottsdale: 480-312-5000

Tempe: 480-350-8311

Mesa: 480-644-2211

Gilbert: 480-503-6500

Chandler: 480-782-4132

Glendale: 623-930-3000

Surprise: 623-222-4000

Peoria: 623-773-8311

Sun City and Sun City West: 623-972-2555

Sedona: 928-282-3100

As an unincorporated part of Maricopa County, the Sun Cities are protected by the Maricopa County Sheriff's Office; a volunteer Sheriff's Posse handles non-emergency calls.

Many towns have information centers like this one in downtown Phoenix

Desert Botanical Garden at Sunset

AREA CODES

Until the late 1990s, the Valley had one area code; however, with the rapid growth of Phoenix and its surrounding cities came two new ones. The original 602 area code covers most of the city of Phoenix. Generally, the East Valley—including Tempe, Scottsdale, Mesa, Gilbert, Chandler, Fountain Hills, and Paradise Valley— uses 480. And the West Valley, including Glendale, Peoria, Surprise, and the Sun Cities (Sun City and Sun City West), is serviced by area code 623. Sedona's area code is 928.

BANKS AND AUTOMATED TELLER MACHINES (ATMS)

As a major metropolitan city, Greater Phoenix supports major banking institutions including Chase Bank, Bank of America, and Wells Fargo. Finding an ATM machine is as easy as heading to the local 7-Eleven, Circle K, or gas station; most have ATM machines inside.

CLIMATE, WEATHER & WHAT TO WEAR

The average temperature in the Valley of the Sun is about 85 degrees Fahrenheit, with the sun shining three-hundred-plus days a year and annual rainfall averaging little more than 8 inches. Depending on the season, temperatures can range from 90 degrees during the day to 60 in the evenings. If you're planning activities that will have you outdoors a good part of the day, it is best to dress in layers. You'll find that you may need a sweatshirt during the cooler morning or evening, while shorts and a T-shirt may suffice during the hottest hours. If you're planning activities that will take you between indoors and outdoors, consider a light jacket or sweater that you can easily put on or take off and carry with you—even during the hottest months. The Valley may be one of the few places in the nation where you go *outside* to warm up; buildings keep the air-conditioning fairly high to combat the heat and the sun, so you may find yourself chilled indoors even if the temperature is over 100 outside.

The Valley has four seasons: spring (mid-February to May 1), summer (May 1 to mid-September), fall (mid-September to late November), and winter (December to mid-February). Spring temperatures range from about 50 to 75 degrees—but it's been known to reach the high 80s and 90s the closer it gets to May. The wonderful part is that once the sun sets, the temperatures drop to a more comfortable level, and light jackets and slacks are often necessary. Summer in the Valley is broken into two mini seasons—dry and rainy. Both are hot, with temperatures over 100 most days and sometimes as high as 110 to 113. May and June tend to be drier, while July, August, and even September are muggier and wetter as thunderstorms sweep through the Valley. Sleeveless shirts, shorts, sandals, and lots of sunscreen are recommended, as are hats and sunglasses during the summer months (sunscreen, hats, and sunglasses are useful in warding off sunburn and headaches all year). Find a pool and get in, but remember to drink lots of water at this time of year—you may not notice that you're sweating, but you are. Temperatures start dropping in late September, when the nights begin to cool off; as October approaches, the days do, too. Much of September has temperatures close to 100 degrees; in October, however, you'll find them closer to 80 and 90, with the evenings dropping to around 60 or 70. November drops to the 70s during the day and the 50s in the evenings. Winter is by far the coolest time of the year; though temperatures rarely drop below freezing even at night, it can and does still hap-

Snow-covered red rocks in Sedona

Phoenix skyline from Piestewa Peak

pen. January and February tend to be rainy and cool. However, the days are often pleasant, with temperatures hovering in the 60s; evenings can fall to as low as the low 40s.

For more information about the weather in the Valley, call the National Weather Service forecast office at 602-275-0073 or visit www.wrh.noaa.gov /Phoenix.

But It's a Dry Heat!

The "dry heat" people think about when they think Phoenix is not altogether a myth. Low humidity make higher temperatures more comfortable; 80-degree weather here may not even be noticeably warm. The mugginess often associated with summers in the Midwest and Southeast only arises during the wet months of July and August, when torrential rains can drench the Valley on a moment's notice. Temperatures in June, July, August, and even September are still very hot; it is not uncommon for the Valley to experience an average of almost 90 days of 100-plus-degree temperatures each summer.

Sun Protection

Keep in mind that even in cooler months the sun is bright, and sunscreen, hats, and sunglasses are useful in preventing sunburn and headaches, which can ruin the rest of your vacation. Reapply sunscreen as directed.

Water

Common signs that your body may be overheating include nausea, vomiting, headaches, fatigue, weakness, and mental fuzziness. The best way to combat heat illness is to proactively drink lots of water. And when you think you've had enough, drink some more. It is not uncommon to see locals carrying water bottles wherever they go. Even during the cooler months, you will need to drink more water than usual—especially if you're exercising. It bears repeating: you may not notice that you're sweating since moisture evaporates so quickly, but you are. That gritty feeling on your skin after prolonged exposure to the heat is the salt left over after your sweat has evaporated. Paying attention to your body and its warning signs is key to enjoying your stay in the desert.

ONLINE RESOURCES

With the power of the Internet growing in leaps and bounds, I'd be remiss not to mention some of the fantastic resources you can find online. While no one source is going to give you the kind of overview a travel guide can, each of these sites and sources can provide additional details and new ideas about what to see and do and where to eat. If you have favorites or come across resources not listed here (or find an update, typo, etc.), drop me a line at christine@christinekbailey.com.

Blogs
Travel blogs, especially the following ones, can be excellent sources of information:

Phoenix Rail Food (www.phxrailfood.com). Provides great information about restaurants along the light rail line, including where to get off and how far you might have to walk. You can also sort by light rail stop or cuisine.

Arizona Travel & Adventure (www.arizonatravelandadventure.com). Updated several times a week by three Arizona travel writers, this blog is constantly offering new things to do and places to go across the entire state—from art walks to off-road rides to where to stay and where to eat.

Buy locally at Phoenix Urban Grocery & Wine Bar

For those of you married to your iPhones, consider supplementing your travel material with the following Arizona iPhone apps:

Family-Friendly Phoenix (http://itunes.apple.com/us/app/family-friendly -phoenix/id355209803?mt=8).

Fire & the Belly (http://fireandthebelly.blogspot.com) Written by Phoenix-based food and drink writer, Geri Koeppel (follow her on twitter at GeriKoeppel), this food blog offers up wonderfully, honest (and often entertaining) reviews on restaurants in the Valley.

Free & Budget Phoenix (http://sutromedia.com/apps/Free_Budget_Phoenix).

Sedona's Scenic Red Rocks (http://sutromedia.com/apps/Sedonas_Scenic _Red_Rocks)

Upcoming travel apps include Greater Phoenix Dining (cafes, restaurants, bar & grills, coffeehouses, winebars, and bistros across the Valley) and Essential Phoenix (a guide to Metro Phoenix's best of the best). Check our joint travel blog—www .ArizonaTravelandAdventure.com—for links to the area's best travel applications for your iPhone!

Twitter
Twitter has proven itself a great resource for discovering a new or even familiar place. Here are a few people who tweet regularly about the people and places mentioned in this book:

ArizonaDOT	LocalFirstAZ	SedonaChamber
ArizonaWeather	MesaThingsToDo	sedonavacation
AZGhostLady	MetroRail	SeeTheSouthwest
azhighways	PhoenixMagazine	ShayWren
AZTouristNews	PhoenixMetro	smithtempe
bikelady	PhoenixPicks	SteveLevineEnt
BruceLeadbetter	PHXRailFood	theazadventurer
ChandlerArts	PHXSkyHarbor	theaztraveler
ChandlerNews	PrescottTourism	TucsonWeekly
DowntownTempe	RailLife	VisitPhoenix
GilbertTownSq	ScottsdaleAZ	VVWineTrail
GlendaleAZ	Scottsdale5thAv	

Also check Twitter for your favorite restaurants, hotels, museums and attractions; most have accounts and offer info on upcoming events, discounts, tips and suggestions.

RECOMMENDED READING
Apache Junction and the Superstition Mountains highlights the mysterious Superstition Mountains and the city at its feet, including the legend of the Lost

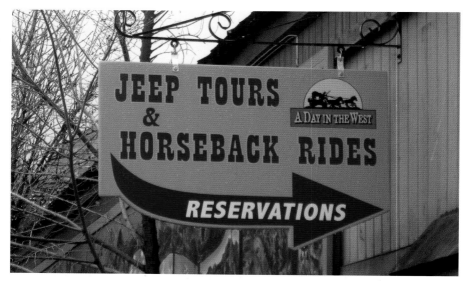

Book a tour in Sedona

Dutchman Mine; it's by award-winning author Jane Eppinga, who has written multiple books about Arizona and its sometimes shady past. Other Eppinga books include *Arizona Sheriffs: Badges and Bad Men* (a historical look at the precarious balance of good and evil in the Wild West) and *Arizona Twilight Tales* (spook stories and haunting tales about our state).

Arizona son and state historian Marshall Trimble takes readers through the history of Arizona from prehistoric tribes to statehood in *Arizona: A Cavalcade of History*. Other Trimble books include *Arizona Trivia* (tidbits about history, entertainment, geography, and sports) and *Arizoniana* (the history of "old Arizona").

The good, the bad, and the ugly are represented in *Arizona Politicians* by James W. Johnson and David Fitzsimmons, published in 2002. For a nonfiction murder mystery, check out *Trunk Murderess: Winnie Ruth Judd* by Phoenix journalist and author Jana Bommersbach, which recounts one of the most legendary crime sagas in Arizona history: did Judd really murder her three friends and ship them off to California in a trunk?

As the fourth-largest city in the state in one of the fastest-growing areas of the Valley, Glendale has risen to the challenge of becoming a mover and shaker. Now home of the Phoenix Coyotes (NHL) and the Arizona Cardinals (NFL), Glendale hosted the Super Bowl in 2008. Find out more about how this little city grew up in the historic account *Glendale* by Carol J. Coffelt St. Clair and Charles S. St. Clair.

Phoenix Then and Now by Paul Scharbach and John H. Akers is an amazing photographic journey through the yesteryears of Phoenix. Side by side sit then-and-now photos of some of the city's most famous sites, such as the San Carlos Hotel, the Heard Building, and the Orpheum Theatre.

Take the time to wander through the desert with *50 Hikes in Arizona*. Martin Tessmer presents a variety hikes, from the urban trails of Phoenix and Tucson to hikes through the Grand Canyon and everywhere in between. With an elevation range of 70 to 12,700 feet, the state has a lot to offer—pine forests, waterfalls, canyons, cacti, and snow!

Find the best fishing spots in the state, including highlights of Arizona's urban lakes, in G. J. Sagi's *Fishing Arizona.* You can also check out the *Game and Fish Water Maps*, which maps more than seven hundred sites, including the Arizona Game & Fish Department's game water catchments, springs, potholes, seeps, and habitat enclosures.

Experience the essence of Arizona's past in the ghost towns and historical haunts that are quickly fading in the desert sun—*Ghost Towns and Historical Haunts of Arizona* by Thelma Heatwole can guide you. Or wander Arizona's hidden highways through the small towns, ghost towns, and the other spaces of the forgotten past along with *Hidden Highways in Arizona* by Richard Harris.

Take to the mountains on your bike. *Mountain Biking Phoenix* by Bruce Grubbs presents 35 of the area's best rides.

For back-road trips around the state, read Jackie Dishner's *Arizona Backroads & Byways,* and for great escapes around the state with or without your family, read *Great Escapes: Arizona* by Teresa Bitler.

Arizona Curiosities (Quirky Characters, Roadside Oddities & Other Offbeat Stuff) presents the quirkier side of the Valentine State. Find silly facts and weird stuff in this funny look at Arizona by author Sam Lowe. For some more of the weird stuff you're bound to find out about Arizona, check out *Weird Arizona: Your Travel Guide to Arizona's Local Legends and Best Kept Secrets* by Wesley Treat.

TOURIST INFORMATION

Arizona Office of Tourism (602-364-3700; www.azot.com), 1110 W. Washington, Suite 155, Phoenix.

Apache Junction
Apache Junction Chamber of Commerce (480-982-3141; www.apachejunction coc.com), 567 W. Apache Tr., Apache Junction.

Carefree & Cave Creek
Carefree/Cave Creek Chamber of Commerce (480-488-3381; www .carefreecavecreek.org), 748 Easy St., Suite 9, Carefree.

Chandler
Chandler Office of Tourism (480-782-3037; www.visitchandler.com).

Chandler Fashion Center, a division of Chandler Visitors Center (480-812-8488), 3111 W. Chandler Blvd., Chandler.

Chandler Chamber of Commerce, Information Center (480-963-4571; www .chandlerchamber.com), 25 S. Arizona Pl., Suite 201, Chandler.

Fountain Hills
Fountain Hills Chamber of Commerce (480-837-1654; www.fountainhills chamber.com), 16837 E. Palisades Blvd., Fountain Hills.

Bar Patio at Trader Vic's in Scottsdale

Photo courtesy of Hotel Valley Ho

Gilbert
Gilbert Chamber of Commerce (480-892-0056; www.gilbertaz.com), 119 N. Gilbert Rd., Suite 101, Gilbert.

Glendale
Glendale Office of Tourism & Visitor Center (623-930-4500; www.visitglendale .com), 5800 W. Glenn Dr., Suite 140, Glendale.

Glendale Chamber of Commerce, Information Center (623-937-4754; www .glendaleazchamber.org), 7105 N. 59th Ave., Glendale.

Mesa
Mesa Convention and Visitors Bureau (480-827-4700; www.mesacvb.com), 120 N. Center, Mesa.

Peoria
Peoria Chamber of Commerce (623-979-3601; www.peoriachamber.com), 8765 West Kelton Lane, Bldg C-1, Peoria.

Phoenix
Downtown Phoenix Visitor Information Center (602-254-6500 or 877-CALL-PHX; www.visitphoenix.com), 125 N. Second Street, Suite 120, Phoenix (across from the main entrance of the Hyatt Regency Phoenix). Open Mon.–Fri. 8–5.

Scottsdale

Scottsdale Convention and Visitors Bureau (480-421-1004; www.scottsdale cvb.com), Galleria Corporate Center, 4343 N. Scottsdale Rd., Suite 170, Scottsdale. Open Mon.–Fri. 8–5.

Visitor Services, Scottsdale Fashion Square Mall, Main Concierge Desk, 7014 E. Camelback Rd., Scottsdale. Open Mon.–Sat. 10–4; Sun. 11–4.

Sedona

Sedona Chamber of Commerce (928-204-1123; www.sedonachamber.com), P.O. Box 478, Sedona, AZ 86339.

Visitor Information Center (928-282-7722 or 800-288-7336), 331 Forest Rd., Sedona. Open Mon.–Sat. 8:30–5, Sun. and holidays 9–3; closed Thanksgiving, Christmas, and New Year's.

Visit Sedona (www.visitsedona.com).

Sun City

Sun City Visitor Center (623-997-5000; www.suncityaz.org), 16824 N. 99th Ave., Sun City.

Surprise

Surprise Regional Chamber of Commerce (623.583.0692; www.surpriseregional chamber.com), 16126 N. Civic Center Plaza, Surprise.

The 411 in Scottsdale

Photo courtesy of Nolan Bailey

Tempe's Winter Festival of the Arts at nightfall

Tempe

Tempe Convention & Visitors Bureau (480-894-8158; www.tempecvb.com), 51 W. Third St., Suite 105, Tempe.

Tempe Chamber of Commerce, Information Center (480-967-7891; www.tempe chamber.org), 909 E. Apache Blvd., Tempe.

ASU Visitor Center, Information Center (480-965-0100; www.asu.edu/vppa /visitorinfo), 826 E. Apache Blvd., Tempe.

TOWN GOVERNMENTS

Chandler (480-782-2200; www.chandleraz.gov), 55 N. Arizona Pl., Suite 301, Chandler.

City of Glendale (main switchboard, 623-930-2000; www.glendaleaz.com), 5850 W. Glendale Ave., Glendale.

City of Mesa (480-644-2011; www.cityofmesa.org), P.O. Box 1466, Mesa, AZ 85211.

City of Phoenix, Phoenix City Hall (city operator, 602-262-6011; www.phoenix .gov), 200 W. Washington St., Phoenix.

City of Sedona (928-204-7127; www
.sedonaaz.gov), 102 Roadrunner Dr.,
Sedona.

City of Tempe (city operator, 480-967-
2001; www.tempe.gov), 31 E. Fifth St.,
Tempe.

Gilbert (480-503-6871; TDD 711;
www.ci.gilbert.az.us), 50 E. Civic
Center Dr., Gilbert.

Peoria, City of Peoria Municipal
Complex (623-773-7000; www.peoriaaz
.gov), 8401 W. Monroe St., Peoria.

Lower cliff dwelling at Tonto National Park

Scottsdale (city manager, 480-312-
2800; general city information, 480-
312-6500; www.scottsdaleaz.gov), 3939 N. Drinkwater Blvd., Scottsdale.

Surprise (623-222-1000; TTY 623-222-1002; www.surpriseaz.com), 16000 N. Civic
Center Plaza, Surprise.

Tanque Verde Ranch in the Rincon Mountains in Tucson

Index

A

"A" Mountain, 124

accommodations: Carefree, 89–90; Casa Grande, 184–85; Chandler, 115; Flagstaff, 191; Fountain Hills, 90; Glendale, 140; Goodyear, 140–41; Jerome, 189; Litchfield, 140–41; Mesa, 114–15; Paradise Valley, 83–84; Peoria, 140; Phoenix, 45, 47–51; Scottsdale, 84–89; Sedona, 159–63; Tempe, 109, 111–14; Tubac, 193–94; Village of Oak Creek, 160. *See also specific accommodations*

Actors Theatre, 61

Adventures Out West, 67–68

Aerospace Maintenance and Regeneration Center (AMARC), 187

Agave Spa at Westin Kierland, 96

Air and Space Museum, Pima, 187

Air Show, Luke Days, 139

airlines, 33

Airport Rental Car Center, 40

airports, 32–34; car rentals, 40; shuttles, 33, 34

AJ's Café, 117

Alice Cooper'stown, 52

Allegiant Air, 34

Aloft Tempe, 113–14

Alta Trail, 74

Amara Hotel, Restaurant & Spa, 162; restaurants, 164–65

ambulances, 199

American Indians: casino accommodations, 90; history of, 20–22, 24–25. *See also specific Indian tribes*

"A" Mountain, 124

AMTRAK, 34

Anaheim Angels, 135

Antique Haven (Glendale), 143

antiquing: Glendale, 143; Scottsdale, 93

Apache Cultural Museum, 192

Apache Indians, 21, 23, 27, 183, 192

Apache Junction Chamber of Commerce, 207

Apache National Forest, 192

Apache Trail, 181, 183

Apple Tree, The, 143

Aqua Fria Freeway (Loop 101), 39

aquariums, 66, 152

Arboretum at Flagstaff, 191

Arcadia Farms, 92–93

Arcosanti, 192

area codes, 201

Arizona Authors and Adventurers, 28

Arizona Biltmore, 50–51

Arizona Biltmore Golf Club, 78

Arizona Broadway Theatre, 150

Arizona Canal, 71

Arizona Cardinals, 79, 153, 154

Arizona Center, 77; restaurants, 53–54

Arizona Climbing and Adventure School (ACAS), 69

Arizona Counter Terrorism Information Center, 199

Arizona Department of Emergency Management, 199

Arizona Department of Public Safety, 199

Arizona Diamondbacks, 28, 79, 107

63–65; history of, 24–28; information, 208; maps, 46, 47; neighborhoods, 14, 16–17; outdoor activities, 67–75, 78; restaurants, 52–59, 62–63; shopping, 76–78; short-trip (48 hours) itinerary, 60–63; spectator sports, 78–79; transportation, 31–34, 43; wine bars, 59. *See also* downtown Phoenix
Phoenix Art Museum, 62, 65, 67, 130
Phoenix City Hall, 210
Phoenix Convention Center, 47
Phoenix Coyotes, 79, 153
Phoenix First Friday Art Walk Downtown, 54, 68
Phoenix International Raceway, 79, 153
Phoenix Marriott Mesa, 115
Phoenix Mercury, 79
Phoenix Mountains Park, 61, 75
Phoenix Open, 106–7
Phoenix Police Department Information Desk, 199
Phoenix Public Library, 68
Phoenix Public Market, 59
Phoenix Rail Food, 204
Phoenix Rock Gym, 132
Phoenix St. Patrick's Day Parade, 125
Phoenix Sky Harbor International Airport. *See* Sky Harbor International Airport
Phoenix Suns, 79
Phoenix Symphony, 61
Phoenix Theatre, 67
Phoenix Visitor Information Center, 208
Phoenix Zoo, 66
Phoenix-Mesa Gateway Airport, 34
Piestewa Peak, 61, 75, 124
Piestewa Peak Parkway (AZ 51), 39
Pillsbury Wine Company, 190
Pima Air and Space Museum, 187
Pima Canyon, 73
Pima Indians, 21–22. *See also* Salt River Pima-Maricopa Indian Community
Pinetop, 192
Pink Jeep Tours, 168–70, 175
Pinnacle Peak Park, 69, 105
pizza (pizzerias), 53, 60, 120, 189
Pizzeria Bianco, 53, 60, 120
planetariums, 129, 130, 150
Pleasant Lake, 71, 151
Poco Diablo Resort, 160
Pointe Hilton Squaw Peak Resort, 49
Pointe Hilton Tapatio Cliffs Resort, 49
Poison Control, 199
police, 199–200
Ponderosa Stables, 151

Praying Monk, 69
Prescott, 192–93
Prescott National Forest, 188–89, 192
Professor Hall's Cinema Museum, 193
Promenade Shopping Center, 106
psychic readings, 178
Pueblo Grande Museum and Archaeological Park, 66

Q
Queen Creek Olive Mill, 118
Quiessence, 57, 58

R
Radisson Fort McDowell Resort & Casino, 90
Rainbow Ryders, 67
Ramada Loop Trail, 75
Ranger Trail, 74
Raven Golf Club at South Mountain, 78
Raven Golf Club at Verrado, 153
Rawhide Wild West Town, 66
reading, recommended, 205–7
Reata Pass Steakhouse, 91–92
Red Mountain Freeway (Loop 202), 39
Red Rock Jeep Tours, 168–69, 175
Red Rock Pass, 172
Red Rock Ranger District, 172; Visitor Contact Center, 172–73
Red Rock State Park, 172, 175
Red Rock-Secret Mountain Wilderness Area, 172
Red's Steakhouse, 148
Renaissance Glendale Hotel & Spa, 140
René, 164
Residence Inn by Marriott Phoenix NW/Glendale, 140
restaurants: Carefree, 58; Chandler, 117; Flagstaff, 191; Gilbert, 58, 118; Glendale, 141–42, 146, 148; Goodyear, 142–43; Jerome, 189; Litchfield, 142–43; Mesa, 117; Paradise Valley, 58, 91; Peoria, 142; Phoenix, 52–59, 62–63; Prescott, 192; Queen Creek, 118; Scottsdale, 91–94; Sedona, 164–65, 168, 169; Tempe, 58, 116–17, 125, 126–27; Tubac, 194; Village of Oak Creek, 164. *See also specific restaurants*
Retreat and Heal, 178
Ride the West, 194
Rincon Mountain District, 188
Rio Salado Habitat Restoration Area, 72
Ritz-Carlton Phoenix, 51; restaurants, 56
Robbins, Marty, 139, 144
rock climbing, 69–70, 132